Revise

Business Studies

David Floyd

Contents

Specification lists

AQA Business Studies

UNIT	SPECIFICATION TOPIC	CHAPTER REFERENCE	STUDIED IN CLASS	REVISED	PRACTICE QUESTIONS
Module 4 (M4) Marketing and accounting and finance	Market analysis	5.1–5.4			
	Marketing strategy	5.1–5.4			
	Marketing planning	5.1–5.4			
	Company accounts	6.1, 6.2			
	Ratio analysis	6.3			
	Contribution and break-even analysis	6.6			
	Investment decision-making	6.4			
Module 5 (M5) People and management	Communication	7.2			
	Employer/employee relations	7.3–7.5			
	Human resource management	7.1–7.5			
	Productive efficiency	8.2, 8.3			
	Controlling operations	8.3			
	Facilities	8.1			
Module 6 (M6) External influences and objectives and strategy	Economic	1.1, 1.2			
	Governmental	1.3			
	Social and other opportunities and constraints	1.4			
	Impact on firms of a change in size	2.1–2.3, 4.2			
	Business objectives	3.1–3.3, 4.1			
	Business strategy	3.1–3.3			

Examination analysis

The specification for the A2 examination (6131) comprises three unit assessments.

Unit 4	Business decision-making case study based on Modules 4 and 5	1 hr 30 min test	30%
<u>Either:</u> **Unit 5W**	Business report and essay based on any A2 Modules	1 hr 30 min test	30%
<u>Or:</u> **Unit 5C**	Coursework project	Untimed	30%
Unit 6	Case study based on Module 6	1 hr 30 min test	40%

Edexcel Business Studies

UNIT	SPECIFICATION TOPIC	CHAPTER REFERENCE	STUDIED IN CLASS	REVISED	PRACTICE QUESTIONS
Unit 4 (M4) Analysis and decision-making	Sales forecasting	5.4, 6.5			
	New product decisions	5.3, 8.2			
	Probability and decision-making techniques	3.3, 5.2			
	Project management	8.3			
	Cost analysis and decision-making	6.5–6.6			
	Ratio analysis in decision-making	6.3			
	Investment appraisal in long-term decision-making	6.4			
	Employer–employee	7.3–7.5			
Unit 5 (M5) Business planning	The planning process	3.1–3.3, 6.5			
	Business planning	3.1			
	Human resource planning	1.1–1.4, 4.1, 7.1			
	Marketing planning	5.1, 5.2			
	Financial planning	6.1, 6.4–6.5			
Unit 6 (M6) Corporate strategy	Responding to the external environment	1.1–1.2			
	Developing a global strategy	1.2, 2.3			
	Responding to social responsibilities and ethics	1.3, 1.4			
	Strategic decisions	2.1, 3.1–3.2			
	Corporate and organisational culture	4.1			
	Management of change	4.2			

Examination analysis

The specification for the A2 examination comprises three unit assessments.

Unit 4	Compulsory structured questions based on A2 Unit 4	1 hr 30 min test	30%
Unit 5 **Either:** **Or:**	Paper 1 Coursework assignment (3000 words) Paper 2 Unseen case study on A2 Unit 5	Untimed 1hr 30 min test	30% 30%
Unit 6	Pre-seen case study with compulsory questions based on A2 Unit 6	1 hr 30 min test	40%

OCR Business Studies

MODULE	SPECIFICATION TOPIC	CHAPTER REFERENCE	STUDIED IN CLASS	REVISED	PRACTICE QUESTIONS
Unit 2874 (M4) Further marketing	The market	5.1			
	Market planning and research	5.1, 5.2			
	Models of marketing	5.1			
	The marketing mix	5.1–5.4			
Unit 2875 (M5) Further accounting and finance	Perspective and concepts	6.1			
	Sources of finance	6.3			
	Budgeting and costing	6.5			
	Final accounts	6.2, 6.3			
	Accounting for decisions	6.6			
Unit 2876 (M6) Further people in organisations	Communication	7.2, 7.3			
	People at work	4.1, 7.3			
	Management of change	4.2			
	Employer/employee	7.1, 7.3–7.5			
	Methods of remuneration	7.3			
Unit 2877 (M7) Further operations management	Production process	2.1, 8.1			
	Constraints on production	1.1–1.4			
	Costs	6.5, 6.6			
	Productive efficiency	8.1–8.3			
	Technology	8.3			
	Research and development	8.2			
Unit 2878 (M8)	Project	(all sections)			
Unit 2879 (M9)	Thematic enquiry	(all sections)			
Unit 2880 (M10) Business Strategy	Setting corporate objectives	3.1			
	Tools for corporate planning	3.3, 5.1, 5.4, 8.3			
	External influences	1.1–1.4			
	Strategy	4.1, 5.1–5.4, 6.3–6.6, 7.1–7.5, 8.1–8.3			

Examination analysis

The specification for the A2 examination comprises three unit assessments. One option is selected from units 2874, 2875, 2876 and 2877; and unit 2879 is an alternative to 2878.

Unit 2874–7	Two compulsory structured questions based on an unseen case study	1hr 30 min test	30%
Unit 2878	A 4000 word report on the findings from a study of a business problem/decision		
Unit 2879	A report based on a written paper, the theme of which is known in advance to allow preparatory study	1 hr 30 min test	30%
Unit 2880	Four compulsory questions based on a a pre-issued case study	2 hr test	40%

WJEC Business Studies

MODULE	SPECIFICATION TOPIC	CHAPTER REFERENCE	STUDIED IN CLASS	REVISED	PRACTICE QUESTIONS
Unit BS 1 section 3.1 (M1) Objectives and the business environment	Business objectives	3.1, 4.1			
	Impact on business of external influences	1.1–1.4, 2.1			
	Business planning and strategy	3.1, 3.2, 5.1, 6.3			
Unit BS 2 section 3.2 (M2) Marketing	Nature and role	5.1			
	Market research	5.2			
	Marketing plan	3.1, 5.1, 5.3			
	Forecasting	5.4			
Unit BS 2 section 3.3 (M3) Accounting and finance	Budgeting	6.5			
	Business accounts	6.1–6.3			
	Costing and profitability	6.4, 6.5			
	Investment appraisal	6.4			
Unit BS 3 section 3.4 (M4) People in organisations	Human resource planning	7.1			
	Organisation structures	4.1, 4.2, 7.1, 8.3			
	Motivation	7.2, 7.3			
	Employer/employee relations	7.3–7.5			
Unit BS 3 section 3.5 (M5) Operations management	Operational efficiency	2.1, 8.2			
	Quality	3.2, 8.2			
	Technology	8.3			
	Business location	8.1			

Examination analysis

The specification for the A2 examination comprises three unit tests.

Unit BS4	Two part-structured questions to be answered, but not more than one from any of the 5 sections	1 hr 15 min test	30%
Either: **Unit BS5a** **Or:**	One stimulus-response question	1 hr 30 min test	30%
Unit BS5b	Coursework investigative study	Untimed	30%
Unit BS6	Questions based on a case study	1 hr 45 min test	40%

NICCEA Business Studies

MODULE	SPECIFICATION TOPIC	CHAPTER REFERENCE	STUDIED IN CLASS	REVISED	PRACTICE QUESTIONS
Module 4 (M4) Objectives and the business environment, people in organisations, and accounting and finance	The corporate plan	2.1, 3.1, 3.2			
	Decision tree analysis	3.3			
	The economy and business	1.1–1.4			
	The organisation and change	4.2			
	Organisation structure	2.1, 4.1			
	Communication	7.2			
	Motivation	7.2, 7.3			
	Management and conflict	4.2, 7.3			
	Trade unions	7.4			
	Final accounts and interpretation	6.1, 6.2			
	Absorption and marginal costing	6.5, 6.6			
	Investment appraisal	6.4			
Module 5 (M5) Objectives and the business environment, marketing and operations management	The corporate plan	2.1, 3.1, 3.2			
	Decision tree analysis	3.3			
	The economy and business	1.1–1.4			
	The organisation and change	4.2			
	The marketing mix	5.1–5.3			
	Marketing	5.1–5.3			
	Forecasting	5.4			
	Critical path analysis	8.3			
	Research and development	8.2			
	Technology	8.3			

Examination analysis

The specification for the A2 examination comprises three unit assessments.

Unit A2 1	Examination paper	1 hr 40 min test	30%
Unit A2 2	Synoptic examination paper based on an unseen case study	1 hr 40 min test	40%
<u>Either:</u> **Unit A2 3e**	Examination paper based on a pre-seen case study	1 hr 40 min test	
<u>Or:</u> **Unit A2 3c**	Coursework (4 000 words in length)	Untimed	30%

AS/A2 Level Business Studies courses

AS and A2

All Business Studies courses being studied from September 2000 are in two parts, with the three separate modules in A2 following on from the three at AS level. Students first study the AS (Advanced Subsidiary) course. The Advanced Subsidiary is assessed at the standard expected halfway through an A Level course: i.e., between GCSE and Advanced (A2) GCE. This means that the new AS and A2 courses are designed so that difficulty steadily increases:

- AS Business Studies builds from GCSE Business Studies
- A2 Business Studies builds from AS Business Studies.

How will you be tested?

Assessment units

At AS Business Studies, you will have been tested by three assessment units. For the full A Level in Business Studies, you will take a further three units. A2 Business Studies forms 50% of the assessment weighting for the full A Level.

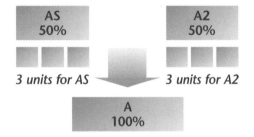

Each unit can normally be taken in either January or June. Alternatively, you can study the whole course before taking any of the unit tests. There is a lot of flexibility about when exams can be taken, and the diagram below shows just some of the ways that the assessment units may be taken for AS and A Level Business Studies.

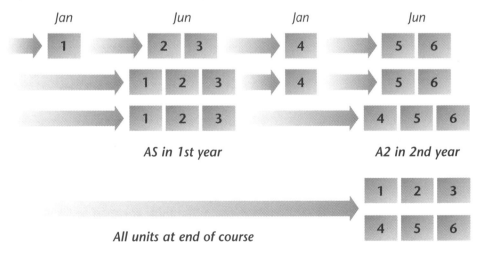

If you are disappointed with a module result, you can resit each module once. You will need to be very careful about when you take up a resit opportunity because you will have only one chance to improve your mark. The higher mark counts.

A2 and Synoptic assessment

Now that you have studied AS Business Studies, by continuing your study of Business Studies to the full A Level you will need to take three further units of Business Studies. Similar assessment arrangements apply, except some units, those that draw together different parts of the course in a 'synoptic' assessment, have to be assessed at the end of the course. Synoptic assessment tests your ability to apply knowledge, understanding and skills you have learnt throughout the course, and to make business decisions and/or solve business problems.

All examination boards therefore set synoptic assessment. The details for each board are summarised on pages 4–8, and we include a detailed example of synoptic assessment in Chapter 9. This assessment forms at least 20% of the overall A Level marks: i.e., 40% of your overall A2 assessment. You can normally expect to sit an examination paper that uses appropriate business themes such as liquidity, human resources or efficiency to integrate the subject-matter you have studied, and to provide a basis for questions that make you draw upon your knowledge of a wide range of business studies topic areas.

Key skills

It is important that you develop your key skills throughout your AS and A2 courses. These are important skills that you need whatever you do beyond AS and A2 Levels. To gain the key skills qualification, which is equivalent to an AS Level, you will need to collect evidence together in a 'portfolio' to show that you have attained Level 3 in Communication, Application of Number and Information Technology. You will also need to take a formal testing in each key skill. It is a worthwhile qualification, as it demonstrates your ability to put your ideas across to other people, collect data and use up-to-date technology in your work.

You will have many opportunities during A2 Business Studies to develop your key skills. Business Studies specifications also provide opportunities for you to produce evidence for assessing the key skills of Improving Own Learning and Performance, Working with Others, and Problem-Solving.

What skills will I need?

Business Studies A Level specifications encourage you to:
- develop a critical understanding of organisations, their internal structure and the external environment in which they operate
- study and analyse business from a number of different perspectives
- acquire a range of skills, including decision-making and problem-solving
- be aware of changes and developments in business life and practice.

For A2 Business Studies, you will be tested by assessment objectives: these are the skills and abilities that you should have acquired by studying the course, and have an equal weighting for the whole A Level qualification. The assessment objectives for A2 are the same as those for AS Business Studies, as follows:

1 demonstrate knowledge and understanding of the specified content
2 apply knowledge and critical understanding to problems and issues arising from both familiar and unfamiliar situations
3 analyse problems, issues and situations
4 evaluate, distinguish between fact and opinion, and assess information from a variety of sources.

Your final A Level grade depends on the extent to which you meet these assessment objectives. This is explained further on page 15.

Different types of questions in A2 examinations

In A2 Business Studies examinations, different types of question are used to assess your abilities and skills. Unit tests mainly use structured questions requiring both short answers and more extended answers. These questions are often linked directly to a given context, requiring you to read and study the stimulus material (a paragraph or short article about a real or imagined business situation).

Short-answer questions

These are sometimes set at AS Level, but are rarely found at A2 because they tend to test recall rather than full understanding of the topic.

Structured questions

Structured questions are quite popular at AS Level, and may also be set at A2 Level. They are in several parts, which may have a common context, and may become progressively more demanding as you work your way through the question. Some of the practice questions in this book are structured questions.

Here is an example of a structured question at A2 Level.

(a) From the employer's perspective, put the case for and against the
    value of trade unions in the workplace.   [8]

(b) 'Enlightened companies treat human resources as their most important
    asset, they provide good conditions of work and reward their workforce
    with higher than average wages.'

    Given the existence of such companies, discuss the view that trade
    unions are no longer necessary.   [12]

WJEC Specimen Paper

When answering structured questions, do not feel that you have to complete one part before starting the next. The further you are into a question, the more difficult the marks are to obtain. If you run out of ideas, go on to the next part/question. You need to respond to as many parts to questions on an exam paper as possible. You will not score well if you spend so long trying to perfect the first questions that you do not reach later questions at all.

Extended answers

At A2 Level Business Studies, questions requiring more extended answers may form part of structured questions, or may form separate questions. At A2, these are often linked to a 'scenario', or case study. These questions are often used to assess your abilities to communicate ideas, to relate your knowledge to the case study, and to assemble a logical argument.

The 'correct' answers to extended questions are often less well-defined than those requiring shorter answers. Examiners may have a list of points for which credit is awarded up to the maximum for the question.

An example of a question requiring an extended answer is shown on page 101.

Points that the examiners might look for in the answers to part (iii) relating specifically to debentures include:

- Positive effects of using debentures – gearing is low enough, there is no potential loss of control, all share capital has already been issued.
- Negative effects of using debentures – have to pay interest, have to repay debentures in the future.

Marks for your answer may be allocated as follows:

12–18 You have discussed at least eight points, including debentures and leasing, and have made a final judgement.

8–11 You have discussed at least six points, including debentures and leasing, and made a final judgement.

4–7 You have discussed at least four points but may not have reached a final judgement, and may have concentrated on debentures or leasing but not both.

1–3 You have mentioned one or two points very superficially, and have probably not made a final judgement.

The quality of your written communication will be assessed in all questions. Marks will be allocated for legible text with accurate spelling, punctuation and grammar, and for a clear, well-organised answer in which you use specialist terms effectively.

Coursework

Coursework may form part of your A Level Business Studies course, depending on which specification you study. You are normally asked to investigate some aspect of business activity. An example of coursework is as follows: you are asked to study how and why a firm has reorganised its manufacturing or service business. In undertaking this coursework, you could consider:

- the reasons behind the reorganisation
- the reorganisation plan
- staff resistance to change
- the change in communications
- how successful the reorganisation has been.

Your coursework will be assessed using the Business Studies assessment objectives described above. Assessment of your coursework includes the use you have made of the key skills you have developed during the course.

Exam technique

Links from AS Business Studies

Advanced Business Studies builds from Advanced Subsidiary Business Studies. This Study Guide has been written so that you will be able to tackle A2 Business Studies from an AS Business Studies background.

The Study Guide includes important business concepts and information. The 'basics' of some of these have been studied at AS Level, and so references to the relevant sections of the accompanying AS Study Guide are included.

What are examiners looking for?

Examiners use instructions to help you to decide the length and depth of your answer.

State, define, list, outline

These key words requires short, concise answers, often recall of material that you have memorised.

Explain, describe, discuss

Some reasoning or some reference to theory is needed, depending on the context. Explaining and discussing require you to give a more detailed answer than when you are asked to 'describe' something.

Apply

Here, you must make sure that you relate your answer to the given situation (this is always good practice in Business Studies exams).

Evaluate

You are required to provide full and detailed arguments, often 'for' and 'against', to show your depth of understanding.

Calculate

A numerical answer is required here.

Some dos and don'ts

Dos

Do answer the question.

- No credit can be given for good Business Studies knowledge that is not relevant to the question.

Do use the mark allocation to guide how much you write.

- Writing more than necessary will not result in extra marks.

Do use real-life business-based examples in your answers.

- These often help illustrate your level of knowledge.

Do write legibly.

- An examiner cannot give marks if the answer cannot be read.

Do use correct 'business language'.

- Marks will be lost if you fail to use terms appropriately.

Don'ts

Don't fill up blank spaces on the exam paper.

- If you write too much on one question, you may run out of time to answer some of the others.

Don't contradict yourself.

- Present reasoned arguments for and against.

Don't spend too much time on a part that you find difficult.

- Exam time is limited, and you can always return to the difficult part if you have enough time at the end of the exam.

What grade do you want?

Everyone would like to improve their grades but you will only manage this with a lot of hard work and determination. Your final A Level grade depends on the extent to which you meet the assessment objectives listed on page 10. The hints below offer advice on how to improve your grade.

To achieve a grade A

You have to:

- show in-depth knowledge and critical understanding of a wide range of business theory and concepts
- apply this to familiar and unfamiliar situations, problems and issues, using appropriate numerical and non-numerical techniques
- evaluate effectively evidence and arguments
- make reasoned judgements in presenting appropriate conclusions.

You have to be a very good all-rounder to achieve a grade A. The exams and coursework test all areas of the syllabus, and any weaknesses in your understanding of Business Studies will be found out.

To achieve a grade C

You have to have a good understanding of the aspects shown in the grade A bullet-points, but you will have weaknesses in some of these areas. To improve, you will need to work hard to overcome these weaknesses, and also make sure that you have an efficient and effective exam technique.

What marks do you need?

As a rough guide, you will need to score an average of between 45% and 55% for a grade C, and over 70% for a grade A.

average	75%	65%	55%	45%	35%
grade	A	B	C	D	E

- When you get your early results, identify a realistic target grade for the A Level from your average mark.
- After taking some modules, you may find that you are above your target grade. This can help safeguard against poor performance later on. It can also mean that you set a higher target grade.
- In a modular course, you will need to score consistently across all modules if you are to achieve a top grade.
- If you plan to resit a module, you must prepare afresh if you are to improve your grade. If you do no extra work for a resit, you could score a lower mark and therefore waste your opportunity.
- Don't become over-confident. You are only as good as your last module result, and you will still need to work hard for each exam.

Four steps to successful revision

Step 1: Understand

- Study the topic to be learned slowly. Make sure you understand the logic or important concepts
- Mark up the text if necessary – underline, highlight and make notes
- Re-read each paragraph slowly.

GO TO STEP 2

Step 2: Summarise

- Now make your own revision note summary:
  What is the main idea, theme or concept to be learned?
  What are the main points? How does the logic develop?
  Ask questions: Why? How? What next?
- Use bullet points, mind maps, patterned notes
- Link ideas with mnemonics, mind maps, crazy stories
- Note the title and date of the revision notes
  (e.g. Business Studies: Marketing, 3rd March)
- Organise your notes carefully and keep them in a file.

This is now in **short term memory**. You will forget 80% of it if you do not go to Step 3.
GO TO STEP 3, but first take a 10 minute break.

Step 3: Memorise

- Take 25 minute learning 'bites' with 5 minute breaks
- After each 5 minute break test yourself:
  Cover the original revision note summary
  Write down the main points
  Speak out loud (record on tape)
  Tell someone else
  Repeat many times.

The material is well on its way to **long term memory**.
You will forget 40% if you do not do step 4. **GO TO STEP 4**

Step 4: Track/Review

- Create a Revision Diary (one A4 page per day)
- Make a revision plan for the topic, e.g. 1 day later, 1 week later, 1 month later.
- Record your revision in your Revision Diary, e.g.
  Business Studies: Marketing, 3rd March 25 minutes
  Business Studies: Marketing, 5th March 15 minutes
  Business Studies: Marketing, 3rd April 15 minutes
  ... and then at monthly intervals.

Chapter 1

The external environment

The following topics are covered in this chapter:

- Economic influences
- European Union influences

- Political influences
- Social and other influences

1.1 Economic influences

After studying this section you should be able to:

- state the main objectives of government macro-economic policies
- explain the effect of these policies on firms

Macro-economic policy

AQA	M6
EDEXCEL	M5, M6
OCR	M10
WJEC	M1
CCEA	M4

GDP differs from **gross national product** (GNP): GDP doesn't include net income from abroad, whereas GNP does.

The government's objectives

The performance of the UK economy can be assessed by measuring its **gross domestic product (GDP)**. This represents the total value of the UK economy's output over the course of a year.

The UK government has four main economic objectives:

- to encourage controllable **economic growth**, e.g. by stimulating demand through interest rate cuts
- to control **inflation**, through its monetary policy (interest rates) and fiscal policy (taxes)
- to sustain **employment** (e.g. through its regional policy)
- to keep a stable **balance of payments**, e.g. by encouraging exporters.

The challenge it faces is to **balance** these objectives. As an example, a high level of economic growth creates employment, but may also increase inflation through increasing demand levels and by attracting imports into the UK: a balance of payments deficit may result. In times of recession, low demand levels stimulate competitive action such as cutting prices, thereby lowering inflation but also creating unemployment.

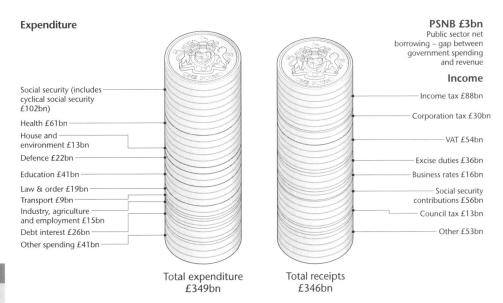

Expenditure

Social security (includes cyclical social security £102bn)
Health £61bn
House and environment £13bn
Defence £22bn
Education £41bn
Law & order £19bn
Transport £9bn
Industry, agriculture and employment £15bn
Debt interest £26bn
Other spending £41bn

Total expenditure £349bn

PSNB £3bn
Public sector net borrowing – gap between government spending and revenue

Income

Income tax £88bn
Corporation tax £30bn
VAT £54bn
Excise duties £36bn
Business rates £16bn
Social security contributions £56bn
Council tax £13bn
Other £53bn

Total receipts £346bn

Figure 1.1 UK government spending and revenue, 1999/2000

Key points from AS

- **Macro-economic issues**
  Revise AS pages 60–63

The effect of macro-economic policy on UK firms

- **Fiscal policy**. Lowering business direct taxes (corporation tax) increases the amount of profit retained and therefore available for re-investment; as firms grow, they increase output and employment. Lowering indirect tax (VAT) will cut prices for consumers, and therefore stimulate demand.
- **Monetary policy**. Lowering interest rates will also stimulate demand, by making capital (and therefore investment) less expensive: firms are more likely to seek to expand by investing, and as a result create more demand for labour. Demand will also be stimulated through consumers having more money to spend as a result of the lowering of their interest rates. Increasing interest rates will increase the cost of borrowing, hitting firms' cashflow through higher interest charges: sales will also be hit, as consumers also face higher bills.
- **Exchange rates**. High UK interest rates will encourage an inward flow of capital (seeking these higher rates) into the UK. As a result, demand for sterling increases, which pushes up its exchange rate. This in turn increases the price of UK exports, making them less competitive, lowering output and therefore affecting employment prospects.

> Joining the single currency will remove the UK government's direct control of monetary policy.

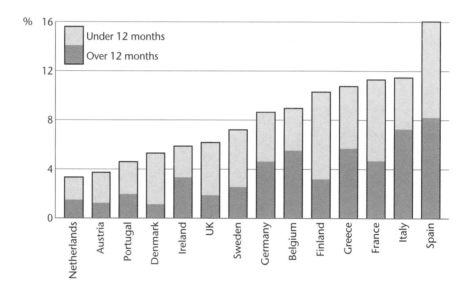

Figure 1.2 *Fighting unemployment in the EU*

Macro-economic policy affects different firms in different ways. Those selling products having a **high income elasticity of demand** (e.g. many luxuries) are often hard hit by a downturn in the economy, with consumers choosing to postpone their purchase of these products. Other firms that produce **capital equipment** are also badly affected, as their customers can't afford – or choose not – to invest in new machinery and equipment.

> In the business cycle – recession, recovery, boom, downturn – personal consumption normally fluctuates less than business investment, which therefore affects different firms in different ways.
>
> **KEY POINTS**

Progress check

1 State the **four** main macro-economic objectives of the UK government.

1 Economic growth; control of inflation; control of unemployment; stable balance of payments.

1.2 European Union influences

LEARNING SUMMARY

After studying this section you should be able to:

- outline the nature and relevance of the EU
- explain the importance of UK firms being part of the EU's Single Market
- present arguments for and against the UK adopting the euro

The Single Market

AQA	M6
EDEXCEL	M6
OCR	M4
WJEC	M1
CCEA	M4

The EU is an example of a **customs union**. It contains four of the G7 group of major industrialised countries (France, Germany, Italy and the UK). The EU was established in 1957 by the Treaty of Rome, and now contains about 400 million consumers in 15 member states.

> The wider **European Economic Area** (EEA) includes EU countries, together with Iceland, Liechtenstein and Norway.

EU membership				
Original members	*Members from 1973*	*Member from 1981*	*Members from 1986*	*Members from 1993*
Belgium	Denmark	Greece	Portugal	Austria
France	Ireland		Spain	Finland
Germany *	United Kingdom			Sweden
Italy				
Luxembourg	* in 1991 the former East Germany was incorporated			
Netherlands				

> Turkey expressed a wish to start negotiating to join the EU, but human rights and other issues delayed this.

Poland, the Czech Republic, Estonia, Slovenia and Cyprus began negotiating in 1998 to join the EU, and have since been joined by Romania, Bulgaria, Slovakia, Malta, Lithuania and Latvia.

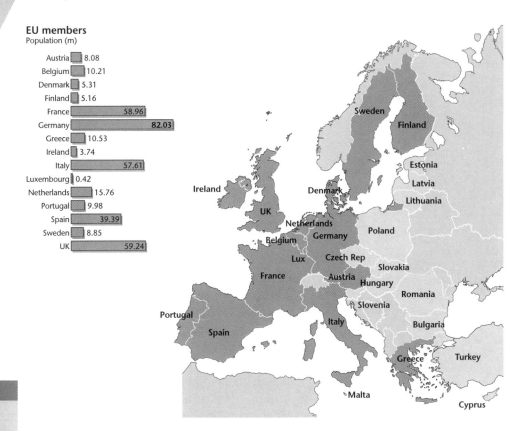

EU members
Population (m)

Austria	8.08
Belgium	10.21
Denmark	5.31
Finland	5.16
France	58.96
Germany	82.03
Greece	10.53
Ireland	3.74
Italy	57.61
Luxembourg	0.42
Netherlands	15.76
Portugal	9.98
Spain	39.39
Sweden	8.85
UK	59.24

Figure 1.3 Possible expansion of the EU

Key points from AS

- **The European Union**
  Revise AS pages 27–28, page 67

The Single Market

Promotion of trade between members was a major reason behind the formation of the then European Community. The 'Common Market' has become the **Single European Market** following the 1986 Single Market Act, which sought to:

remove		*establish*	
	• administrative barriers to trade		• free movement of labour
	• controls on the flow of capital		• free movement of goods
	• the abuse of market power		• common technical standards
			• parity of professional qualifications

Examples of Single Market activity

- The '**New Approach**' – also known as **CE Marking** – Directives set out various requirements (e.g. for safety) that have to be met before products can be sold in member states. Products meeting this requirement carry the CE mark, which means they can be sold anywhere in the Community.
- The EU's **Machinery Directive** requires that all new or imported machinery complies with UK health and safety regulations (this machinery will carry the CE mark).
- The EU's **Social Charter** (page 116) establishes the general principles on which the EU model of labour law and the place of work in society is based.
- The EU's **Competition Policy** seeks to control the number and level of monopolies in its member countries – its **Merger Control Regulation** is designed to ensure that trade in the EU takes place on the basis of free and fair trading.
- Examples of EU Directives on consumer protection include:
  - the **Electronic Commerce Directive**, making information providers give certain information (e.g. name and address, prices) to people using e-commerce
  - the **Doorstep Selling Directive**, which provides a one week 'cooling off' period if certain goods are bought at home
  - the **Toy Safety Directive**, which harmonises toy safety standards
  - the **Misleading Advertising Directive**, which protects against unfair advertising practices
  - the **Price Indication Directive** harmonises the display of selling prices throughout the EU.

The underlying principle behind these and other Directives is the free movement of goods.

Influence of the Single Market on UK businesses

- **Common standards.** Community-wide standards of quality and safety have been established. UK manufacturers must ensure their products meet these EU standards.
- **Open markets.** These now exist in areas such as information technology, telecommunications and financial services. UK firms face increased competition through these open markets with their common standards.
- **Free movement of labour.** The free movement of individuals is one of the EU's basic principles set out in its Social Charter. The increased recognition of professional qualifications between member states affects employment opportunities for UK citizens, and the recruitment policies of UK firms.
- **Free movement of goods.** The use of the SAD (Single Administrative Document) and simplified border formalities reduce delay in moving goods throughout the Union. Transport services have been liberalised, for example by abolishing all road haulage permits and quotas.
- **Regulation of anti-competitive practices.** EU anti-competition rules seek to allow competition to flourish. Between 1990 and 2000, the EU blocked 13 mergers/takeovers for being anti-competitive, including the Airtours bid for First Choice Holidays (1999) and Volvo's bid for Scania trucks (2000).

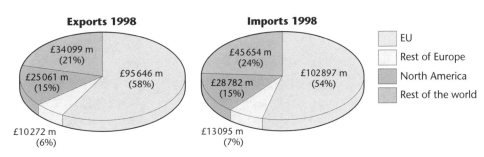

Figure 1.4 *Importance of trade with the EU*

European monetary union (EMU)

AQA	M6
EDEXCEL	M6
OCR	M4
WJEC	M1
CCEA	M4

The four not adopting the euro at the time were Denmark, Greece, the UK and Sweden (Greece joined the euro area in 2001).

On 1 January 1999, eleven member states adopted the **euro** as their common currency. The conversion rates between the euro and national currencies were fixed, the arrangement being to withdraw these currencies in the first half of 2002 and replace them with euro notes and coins. All transactions in the various financial markets – capital, money and foreign exchange – are carried out in euros, with private households having the opportunity of using the euro in cheque and credit card transactions.

The trade of goods and services within the **Eurozone** (the euro area) is no longer 'foreign' trade: it is now domestic trade. Any related balance of payments problems are therefore eliminated for the member states. Exchange rate instability within the euro area is also eliminated.

The euro has led to a transfer of monetary policy from the member countries to the **European System of Central Banks** (ESCB – see below). As a result, using interest and exchange rates to help control national monetary policy is no longer available to the member governments. There is, therefore, in the Eurozone, a single currency and a single monetary policy.

The European System of Central Banks (ESCB)

Because of its independence, the ESCB will in practice have to report to the European Parliament, the Commission and the European Council.

The ESCB was created in 1998. It is a **supranational** organisation, i.e. it is independent of national governments. The effect of its being independent is to remove monetary policy from the control of the individual governments making up the euro area.

The ESCB's main tasks are to:

*   carry out monetary policy for the euro area
*   conduct foreign exchange transactions
*   manage the official currency reserves of the countries in the euro area.

A major influence on the inflation rate in the euro area will be the differences in real incomes across its members.

The ESCB's main instrument of monetary policy is **open market operations**. The main objective of the ESCB in carrying out its monetary policy is to **maintain price stability**. It has the freedom to define what 'price stability' means in practice, and can follow what it considers to be the most important strategy to achieve this: it can therefore decide what the target is, and how it will be reached. In practice, this will involve supervising the link between inflation and the money supply through:

*   monetary targeting
*   inflation targeting.

> The ESCB is influenced in its work by **Ecofin**, the forum of the EU's finance ministers.
>
> **KEY POINTS**

'Euroland': the Eurozone

Key points from AS

*   **The European Union** *Revise AS pages 27–28, page 67*

The member states adopting the euro have a population slightly larger than that of the USA and more than twice the size of Japan, the world's two other leading economies. Total GDP of the member states equalled some three-quarters that of the USA – $6017 billion compared with $7824 billion – and was double that of Japan ($3100 billion).

The euro
Now in business

Indicator	Date	Original euro area	USA	Japan
Population (millions)	1997	290.4	271.8	126.0
GDP per head ($000)	1997	20.7	28.8	24.6
Inflation (%)	1998	1.3	1.6	0.6
Unemployment (%)	1998	11.0	4.5	4.1

Figure 1.5 Economic indicators for the original euro area, the USA and Japan Source: OECD national statistics.

In practice, the 'big three' economies of France, Germany and Italy dominate, accounting for about three-quarters of the euro area's GDP.

Eurozone member	GDP (1997) (% share)	GDP (1997) (per head) *	Inflation (1998) (%)	Unemployment (1998) (%)
Austria	3.3	118	0.8	4.4
Belgium	3.9	111	0.9	8.8
Finland	1.9	106	1.4	11.8
France	22.3	111	0.7	11.9
Germany	33.3	118	0.7	9.7
Ireland	1.2	92	2.2	7.8
Italy	18.1	92	2.0	12.2
Luxembourg	0.3	175	1.0	2.2
Netherlands	5.8	108	1.8	4.1
Portugal	1.6	47	2.3	4.9
Spain	8.4	62	1.8	18.9
Euro area	100	100	1.3	11.0
* (100 = average euro area)				

Figure 1.6 Euro area statistics   Source: OECD

The euro in foreign exchange transactions

The euro's role as an international investment currency and part of a country's official reserves has not yet developed. It is unlikely to be a serious competitor to the dollar as an international currency in the near future, because of the dollar's wide acceptance and use. The euro is expected to become a major competitor against sterling.

The dollar gains from economies of scale (reduced exchange-related transaction costs) due to its wide use in foreign exchange as the medium of exchange between other currencies.

EMU and the UK

EMU – **Economic and Monetary Union** – is closely associated with the establishment of the Eurozone. The UK government supports the principle of joining if the economic benefits of doing so are clear, and has a dedicated unit in the Treasury – the **Euro Preparations Unit** (EPU) – to help UK firms prepare for the effects of the euro.

The existence of the single currency will influence EU markets in three main ways.

- **Exchange rates**. All uncertainties in exchange rate movements are removed for trade within the euro area when trade is valued in the single currency.
- **Transaction costs**. There is no need to change national currencies in the Eurozone: transaction costs are reduced as a result, and firms find it cheaper to make payments between countries.
- **Transparency**. Price differences will be more transparent as a result of the single currency.

'We see the euro as one of the key drivers of competition in retailing, because it will promote cross-border price transparency and encourage consumers to press for the best value available anywhere in the single market rather than simply in their domestic market.'

Kingfisher (the UK's leading European retailer) chief executive Sir Geoff Mulcahy, 2000

It is likely that those UK firms that prepared early for the euro will have achieved a competitive advantage over their rivals.

The UK businesses most affected by EMU are **exporters** and **importers** who will be forced to deal with the euro, **multinationals** with UK bases (these may use the euro to simplify their accounting procedures), the **financial sector** (banks and other financial institutions, and financial markets), and **retailers** (for example, the major retailers based in tourist areas).

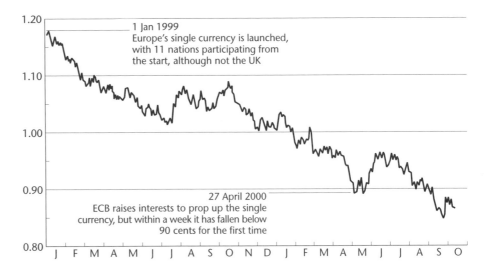

1 Jan 1999
Europe's single currency is launched, with 11 nations participating from the start, although not the UK

27 April 2000
ECB raises interests to prop up the single currency, but within a week it has fallen below 90 cents for the first time

Figure 1.7 Initial performance of the euro against the dollar   *Source: Primark Datastream*

Evidence for and against the UK joining the Eurozone

- Although many manufacturers have faced problems since the euro was established due to the strength of the pound against it, any raw materials they import are very competitively priced as a result.
- Companies like Nissan, Toyota and Ford have either cut jobs, announced closures or warned that future investment is put at risk because of the high rate of sterling against the euro. Although part of their argument that the UK should join the Eurozone may be influenced by other factors such as over-capacity in vehicle production, in 2000:
  - Toyota, Nissan and Honda all reduced their dependence on UK-made components by over 10%
  - Matsushita (makers of Panasonic and National televisions) moved production of its flat-screen TV sets to the Czech Republic, and started importing more TV components from Germany
  - Hitachi ceased making personal computers in the UK
  - Canon cut 200 jobs from a Scottish-based factory
  - Sony cut 400 jobs in South Wales
  - Sumitomo announced the closure of its plant in north-east England.

'We could be interested in limiting output [of Nissan Micra cars] at Sunderland and increasing output at other European plants.'

Carlos Ghosn, Nissan president June 2000 (Nissan Sunderland employed about 5000 staff in 2000)

> 'If Britain does nothing to solve the problem [of the high pound], foreign companies, regardless of whether they are Japanese, American or whatever nationality, may exit the country.'
>
> *Kunio Nakamura, president of Matsushita (employer of about 5000 workers in the UK), August 2000.*

- Concern has therefore been expressed that inward investment will be lost if the UK doesn't join the single currency, although in 1999 there was a record number of new projects generating new inward investment. This investment is thought to have created over 50 000 jobs: the USA was responsible for 48% of these projects, Germany for 8% and Japan for 7.7% *(source: Invest.uk)*. The UK is often seen as a gateway to mainland Europe, and much of this investment would probably be maintained if the UK does not join the single currency in the near future.
- The European Commission has found that UK business is already heavily involved with using the euro: 29% of their international transactions (by volume) in 2000, compared with an EU average of 24%, and some 7% of UK firms held euro bank accounts compared with an EU average of 3%.

UK firms need to consider the extent to which the single currency and euro area will create or affect:

- **increased cross-border competition** – UK firms are disadvantaged compared with Eurozone-based firms that share the same currency
- **raising finance** – euro-based financial markets may become more attractive
- **buying and moving goods** – firms located in the Eurozone should find buying, transport and distribution costs are reduced due to the more transparent competition and the lack of fluctuating exchange rates
- **selling** – pricing UK firms' products in both sterling and euros
- **greater competition from growth or co-operation** – the single currency and increased competition for firms within the euro area may encourage mergers, closer co-operation and joint ventures for these firms.

How Listawood Group Ltd has been influenced by EMU

'Overall, the euro simplifies our business, reduces administration and transport costs and makes it much easier to deal with exchange rate risk. Accordingly, we will trade in the currency as much as we are able... With an annual price list system, we are always going to be vulnerable to changes in exchange rates but now we have just the one euro list, it is much easier to monitor and to be aware of the exact position... The mechanics of setting up euro accounts and contacting customers and suppliers were not difficult or particularly time consuming. Plus, getting ready for the euro has given us a chance to think through our business. Price transparency will undoubtedly have an impact. In some ways, it will make it easier to plan but it is also likely to make Europe a more competitive market.'

KEY POINTS

Three major challenges UK firms face are in changing their **accounting and IT-based systems** to accommodate the euro, having to re-consider their **pricing policies** so that their goods are competitively priced in euros, and having to **train staff** to handle euro-based transactions.

Progress check

1 In what ways does the Single Market influence UK business?
2 How are EU markets affected by establishment of the Eurozone?

1 Establishing common standards; creating open markets; allowing free movement of labour, capital and goods.
2 Removing uncertainties in exchange rates; reducing or eliminating transaction costs; making price differences much more transparent.

1.3 Political influences

After studying this section you should be able to:

● describe the main forms of political influence on UK firms
● explain how these influences can provide opportunities as well as threats

The nature of political influence

AQA	M6
EDEXCEL	M6
OCR	M10
WJEC	M1
CCEA	M5

An example of a politically-based campaign was the criticism in the late 1990s of the pay of some 'fat cat' directors.

An increasingly important trend is for politically-influenced organisations such as pressure groups to create 'virtual' communities of activists through the use of email and the Internet.

A key challenge for managers is to **identify and manage risk**. Managers have traditionally concentrated on risks associated with technology, finance and the market, but increasingly have to consider how **political** influences can seriously disrupt the work of their organisation.

The scope of political influence includes:

● **impact on operations** – e.g. work-based legislation such as the minimum wage, equal pay and non-discrimination will affect cost levels, and political decisions on grants and planning regulations influence location decisions
● **impact on products** – restrictions on product development (e.g. environmental controls, health and safety regulations controlling productive processes and equipment)
● **impact on image** – e.g. the Labour government 1997–2001 had a policy of 'naming and shaming' organisations (e.g. some railway companies, and certain financial sector firms) of which it was critical.

The costs of some of these influences to some firms may also present **opportunities** to others. For example, the introduction of new savings (e.g. ISAs) and pensions (e.g. the new 'stakeholder pension') brings opportunities for firms in the financial services sector; and new regulations controlling environmental waste presents the opportunity for a firm to develop waste- and energy-saving processes (and to market these).

Responding to political influences

Directors may decide to carry out regular **political audits**, to judge the nature and extent of the political risks faced by their firm. They also need to assess expected or actual political influences when making major strategic decisions such as relocation or the manufacture of a new product.

Key points from AS

● **Government support**
  Revise AS pages 64–66
● **Legal regulation**
  Revise AS page 68
● **Competition policy**
  Revise AS page 70

Any **SWOT** analysis, of external opportunities and threats, should include an assessment of politically-based risks and opportunities.

KEY POINTS

1.4 Social and other influences

After studying this section you should be able to:

- *explain the nature and importance of environmental management*
- *assess the value of a firm having a positive ethical policy*

LEARNING SUMMARY

Environmental management

AQA	M6
EDEXCEL	M6
OCR	M10
WJEC	M1
CCEA	M5

The firm can use any improvement in environmental image as an effective marketing tool.

Organisations have become increasingly aware of the impact they have on the environment and their local communities. They can use this impact to gain a competitive advantage, through efficient environmental management.

Specific benefits and financial savings will result from:

- reduced risk of legal action
- improved image
- improved energy efficiency
- better waste management
- improved relationships with actual and potential investors.

> 'Tesco will be one of a small number of companies to meet the Government's recommendation on energy reduction... Our buildings are designed and our equipment is chosen to minimise energy use... We won a *Retail Week* award for energy awareness.'
>
> *Source: Tesco plc annual review 1999*

Carrying out environmental management

An organisation has to consider internal and external influences. **Internally**, the normal procedure is for a firm to carry out three steps, as follows.

- **Undertake an environmental audit** to establish the current level of environmental performance and achievement. To do this, managers and employees assess the firm's present impact on the environment, together with how it is being influenced by current legislation.
- **Create an environmental policy.** This is created as a result of the environmental audit, and often involves documenting environmentally-friendly work procedures, and setting environmental objectives. It will be communicated to all staff, thereby continuing to involve and motivate them.
- **Monitor environmental performance.** Performance can now be measured against set objectives, to improve the firm's environmental performance.

Externally, the organisation will need to consider **supply chain** environmental impacts. It may seek to 'green' the supply chain, which will enable it to publicise or advertise this benefit.

> **Trading Charter**
> 'We will use environmentally sustainable resources wherever technically and economically viable. Our purchasing will be based on a system of screening and investigation of the ecological credentials of our finished products, ingredients, packaging and suppliers.'
>
> *Source: The Body Shop international plc.*

Key points from AS
- **Other influences**
  Revise AS pages 71–72

Sainsbury's and Somerfield consider the environment

'In response to consumer concerns, Sainsbury's Supermarkets became one of the first retail chains to eliminate genetically-modified (GM) ingredients from all its own brand products.'

'Environmental concerns during the year centred on the issue of GM crops. We have removed GM ingredients from all our own label products and do not sell any GM fruit or vegetables.'

Sources: J Sainsbury plc annual report 2000, Somerfield plc annual report 1999/2000

Although there will be financial costs associated with such an environmental management policy, saving waste can also avoid penalties. For example, the EU's **Packaging Waste Directive** has had a major impact on environmentally-inefficient firms' costs, because it imposes charges on those firms that create waste.

Business ethics

AQA	M6
EDEXCEL	M6
OCR	M10
WJEC	M1
CCEA	M5

The ethical behaviour and policy of an organisation will be heavily influenced by the ethical stance of the people who make up that organisation.

'Ethics' refers to a code of morally correct behaviour. Firms nowadays make ethical statements that outline the moral stance they take in business.

Ethical statement concerning the treatment of animals

'We are against animal testing in the cosmetics and toiletries industry. We will not test ingredients or products on animals, nor will we commission others to do so on our behalf. We will use our purchasing power to stop suppliers animal testing.'

Source: The Body Shop International plc.

To clarify the firm's ethical policy, an **ethical code of practice** is normally drawn up. This document outlines the way the firm's employees are expected to behave in certain situations, and will be tailored to the nature of the business. Organisations such as The Body Shop, which take pride in their ethical stance, may concentrate on general human rights issues; manufacturing firms may focus on the environment, financial institutions on honesty and integrity, and so on.

'Shell companies insist on honesty, integrity and fairness in all aspects of their business and expect the same in their relationships with all those with whom they do business… Shell companies act in a socially responsible manner within the laws of the countries in which they operate.'

Source: Extracts from the Statement of General Business Principles of the Royal Dutch/Shell Group of Companies

If firms fail to make a commitment towards acceptable business ethics, there are legal controls available, including the recent **Human Rights Act** (2000). There are also voluntary agreements: for example, in 2000 a voluntary code of practice for multinational companies was agreed by the OECD (Organisation for Economic Co-operation and Development) that incorporates human rights standards. Under the code, a multinational will be held accountable for abuses of its employees and the environment throughout the world.

The Public Interest Disclosure Act has been called the 'Whistleblowers Act'.

Also nowadays, employees can impose their own ethical views to a greater extent. For example, the UK's **Public Interest Disclosure Act** (1999) protects those employees who wish to raise concerns about issues at work. The Human Rights Act (2000) is expected to support the Public Interest Disclosure Act by making employees more comfortable about bringing abuses at work to light.

Key points from AS

- **Other influences**
  Revise AS pages 71–72

Benefits and drawbacks of an ethical policy

The **benefits** from an ethical policy are:

- **Marketing benefits.** A firm may find that many of its customers will only buy its products if it does have an acceptable ethical policy. As a result, having drawn up an ethical code of practice, the firm will normally publish it in order to communicate its policy to customers, and therefore to support its marketing strategy.
- **Employee benefits.** Firms adopting positive ethical practices often find that their employees are more motivated to work for them.

The **problems** associated with an ethical policy include **lower profits**, since ethical behaviour is likely to lead to higher costs, and **conflict with existing objectives** such as profit maximisation and market share. For example, an objective based on profit maximisation policy (e.g. through exploitation of labour or the environment) may encourage the firm to act in a way that should not be acceptable under its ethical policy.

Pressure groups

Many pressure groups, such as **Action on Smoking and Health** (ASH) and the **League Against Cruel Sports**, adopt ethical stances and may seek to encourage certain organisations to adopt a similar viewpoint.

> Although environmental and ethical policies commit the firm to expenditure and will increase overall costs, they are of great benefit to the firm's image and its marketing strategy.

 KEY POINTS

Progress check

1 List the steps in establishing an effective environmental policy.

2 What are the main benefits to a firm from having an ethical policy?

2 Use as part of its marketing strategy; more motivated and committed staff.
1 Undertake an audit; create a policy; monitor achievement; also consider trying to 'green' the supply chain.

Sample question and model answer

1

HavaGo plc is a major retailing 'do-it-yourself' (DIY) store. It is aware that all its major competitors are publicising their ethical policies. The management of HavaGo plc is in the process of reviewing the company's ethical policy to establish a better defined ethical code. As a result of the review, it has been decided to implement a much clearer and more aggressive ethical policy.

(a) What is 'ethical policy' and an 'ethical code'? [4]

(b) Describe **two** types of ethical policy that might be adopted by the managers of HavaGo plc. [6]

(c) Evaluate the costs and benefits of **one** of these policies to the employees of HavaGo plc. [10]

A good answer. We could also include the point that an organisation's ethics are shaped by (a) its culture, and (b) the nature of its business.

(a) 'Ethical policy' refers to the code of behaviour adopted by a business. They give a sort of moral guideline on what it does. An 'ethical code' is the document that actually sets out the way the business and its staff act in certain situations.

This answer includes some relevant policies, although it could outline some relevant illustrations, e.g. by including mention of how anti-discriminatory practices (race, sex and disability) affect specific functions (Human Resources, customer service, shop layout, advertising images, etc.).

(b) The first policy I would recommend is for HavaGo plc to consider the effects of its policies on the environment. It could, for instance, encourage customers to reuse plastic bags, it should only sell 'environmentally-friendly' and 'repeat-use' products where possible, and it shouldn't trade with any firms that exploit their local environment. The second ethical policy I would recommend would be to support equal opportunities. HavaGo should make sure it applies all the UK and EU legislation on anti-discrimination, and it should also support local and national equal opportunities initiatives.

It is important to refer to motivation theory: other theorists such as Herzberg could also be included.

(c) The benefits of Policy 2 to employees are that it will give them a greater sense of worth and self-esteem (Maslow), and the business may also prosper – its enhanced reputation and goodwill lead to positive publicity and more sales, and also help frame advertising campaigns that will again increase sales. If this happens, higher profits should result, which could ensure jobs are secure and also benefit employees through share schemes/profit-sharing.

The cost of this policy to employees is that monitoring and applying laws have a financial cost that will affect HavaGo's profits. Also, prices charged by 'acceptable' suppliers may be higher: as a result, some customers may go elsewhere for lower prices if HavaGo's price competitiveness suffers. This may put pressure on keeping jobs for employees, and reduced profit margins may lead to lower share prices and lower dividends if they are part of an incentive share scheme.

Practice examination questions

1 (a) Explain how organisations might be influenced by an increased awareness
of environmental matters. [10]

(b) NAM Ltd makes components for the vehicle industry. The directors of NAM Ltd
are considering whether to change their policy on how the industrial waste is
disposed of. The company is based in an area formerly used for mining and
quarrying: as a result, this waste is used as 'land-fill' to help fill the old mining
and quarrying sites. The directors are proposing to buy and use large machinery
to crush and burn the waste.

Identify the main costs associated with such a decision. [10]

2 (a) Outline the main advantages, to a company exporting goods from Britain,
of the UK joining the Single European Currency (the euro). [8]

(b) Discuss the reasons why the business community in the United Kingdom
is divided over the issue of joining the Single European Currency. [12]

WJEC Specimen paper BS4

Chapter 2

Business organisations

The following topics are covered in this chapter:

- Business organisations
- The small firm
- Multinationals

2.1 Business organisations

After studying this section you should be able to:

- outline the practical difficulties of starting a business
- explain the differing legal forms of business in the private sector
- identify the methods used by firms to grow in size
- evaluate the problems associated with growth

Starting a private sector business

AQA	M6
EDEXCEL	M5, M6
OCR	M5
WJEC	M5
CCEA	M4

Key points from AS

- **Entrepreneurs and profit**
  Revise AS pages 33–34
- **Legal liability and legal status**
  Revise AS page 34
- **Organisations in the private sector**
  Revise AS pages 36–40
- **Stakeholders**
  Revise AS page 42

Liquidity measures the ability of the firm to meet its debts as they fall due.

Entrepreneurs – risk takers – are willing to take risks in order to make profits. There are many practical difficulties of starting a new business, including:

- **Obtaining sufficient finance** – the **amount** needs careful calculation, and it must be obtained at a **cost** (rate of interest) acceptable to the entrepreneur. **Security** will be required by the lender, which may be difficult to find. The most popular source of finance are the banks, offering loans and/or the facility to overdraw on a business current account.
- **Finding a suitable location** – what is needed is an **affordable site** in a location suitable for employing **staff** (and for their commuting), and for **transport** and **communications** from both a supplier and a customer perspective.
- **Identifying a gap in the market** – all firms depend on a satisfactory demand for their goods and services. As a result, an entrepreneur wishing to establish a new business must try to avoid duplicating a product that is already available at a competitive price, meeting demand in the market.
- **Ensuring adequate cash flow** – bad cash flow management is the most common cause of business failure. **Liquidity** is more important than profitability in the short term, particularly in the early part of a firm's existence.

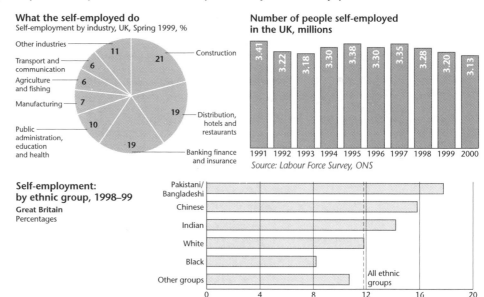

Figure 2.1 Self-employment in the UK

Source: ONS

The legal form of the business

Sole traders remain the most popular form of business in the UK. Both sole traders and partnerships have the drawbacks of **unlimited liability** for their owners, and these forms of business organisation are **unincorporated** since they do not possess a legal existence separate from that of their owners.

Private and public limited companies offer the benefit of **limited liability**. Since, however, their shareholder owners are – especially in a plc – usually distinct from the people who control them (directors), a **divorce of ownership from control** is created. The result is that there will be no guarantee that the directors will always act in the best interests of the shareholders. Other **stakeholders** such as employees, the public and the government, will also influence the directors' actions and decisions.

The limited liability partnership (LLP)

In 2000 the **Limited Liability Partnerships Act** was passed as a result of partners in existing partnerships becoming more concerned with unlimited liability. This new form of business ownership is similar to a limited company, in that:

- the LLP is a **legal person** separate from its members
- it also has to use an abbreviation ('**LLP**') at the end of its name.

It is expected that a number of large professional partnerships, such as accountants and lawyers, may decide to become LLPs.

> The chance to make profit, and the protection afforded by limited liability, make the private limited company a very successful form of business.

KEY POINTS

Size and growth

AQA	M6
EDEXCEL	M5, M6
OCR	M5
WJEC	M10
CCEA	M4

Many organisations adopt **growth** as one of their main business objectives. The organisation may grow **organically**, through internal expansion, or **externally** as a result of merger or takeover. It may also grow through selling its products in **new markets**, and expanding **internationally** (both being linked with organic growth).

The measurements of size – turnover, profits, capital employed, employees – may each give an incomplete picture of the size of the organisation concerned.

> 'Sainsbury's Egypt operates 100 stores, nine of which now bear the Sainsbury's name on their fascia. All are situated in and around the Cairo metro area.'
>
> *Source: J Sainsbury plc annual report 2000*

People's resistance to change (page 58) is a major contributory factor to mergers and takeovers being unsuccessful.

Mergers and **takeovers** remain the most popular way to grow quickly. **Synergy** – 'the whole is greater than the sum of its parts' – has often been used as an argument to justify taking over another business: the specific arguments are the expected gains from **economies of scale**, and a **reduced risk through diversification** of products. In the 1990s, however, there was a growing trend for demergers to take place, often as a result of unsuccessful takeovers or mergers.

Somerfield's assessment of its merger difficulties

'Somerfield is a complex group which has grown by various acquisitions and mergers over the past decades, the biggest of which was the merger with Kwik Save in March 1998. This merger brought significant extra scale to the Group and also substantial synergies in the form of a reduction in the cost of goods... This corporate activity has left the Group with a variety of supply

Key points from AS

- **Size and growth**
  Revise AS pages 52–55
- **Economies of scale**
  Revise AS pages 56–57

chain systems as well as stores ranging from small convenience stores to large supermarkets... Bringing together the two companies' supply chains will bring us valuable economies of scale as we get it right but the first stages of the integration process caused serious disruption last year... By November 1999, the decline in sales drove management to revise its strategy... However, this new plan created further uncertainty, weakened Kwik Save and sales continued to decline. To compound these problems, some cost reduction measures exacerbated the supply chain problems and began to affect Somerfield sales. This year the Board has been able to take a fresh look at the direction of the business.'

Source: Somerfield plc annual report 1999/2000

Possible problems arising from growth include:

- **financial** – expansion brings pressure on the firm's liquidity, e.g. as a result of offering additional credit to encourage sales, and on its level of gearing (page 84)
- **managerial** – although growth may have been planned efficiently by managers, they may find that this growth makes the firm's various functions/projects more difficult to co-ordinate and to control, and its communication procedures slower
- **organisational** – e.g. the growth from private limited to public limited requires the company to float its shares on the stock market. This brings added pressures, e.g. from its share price, and as a result of financial analysts' opinions on the company's performance being expressed publicly
- **international** – there is no guarantee that what is popular in the UK or other home market will become equally popular overseas; there will be many local and national differences (e.g. due to culture); and control and co-ordination become more difficult as a result of international expansion.

International growth can also change local cultures: e.g. the 'Americanisation' of young 'street' fashion throughout much of the world.

McDonald's adapts to overseas cultural requirements

'Out of respect for local cultures, McDonald's restaurants in Arab countries maintain 'Halal' menus, which signify compliance with Islamic laws for food preparation, especially beef... The first kosher McDonald's opened in early 1995 in a suburb of Jerusalem. It does not serve dairy products, and is closed on Saturdays, the Jewish Sabbath. And in India, the Big Mac is made with lamb and is called the Maharaja Mac.'

Source: McDonald's

Diseconomies of scale often set the limits to growth.

KEY POINTS

Progress check

1 What are the four major difficulties associated with starting a business?
2 In what ways do firms grow?

2 Organically; through mergers; by taking over another firm.

1 Obtaining sufficient capital; finding a suitable location; identifying a gap in the market; ensuring adequate cash flow.

2.2 The small firm

After studying this section you should be able to:

- *define what is a 'small' and 'medium sized' firm*
- *describe the problems small firms typically face*
- *explain how small firms continue to survive in the UK economy*

LEARNING SUMMARY

Defining 'small'

AQA	M6
EDEXCEL	M6
OCR	M4
WJEC	M10
CCEA	M4

Accounting definitions of what constitutes **'small'** and **'medium sized'** have been made. To be classified as either small or medium sized, the company needs to meet any two of three conditions based on a single financial year's performance:

	Small	Medium sized
Annual turnover	£2.8 million or below	£11.2 million or below
Balance sheet total assets	£1.4 million or below	£5.6 million or below
Average number of employees	50 or under	250 or under

Small and medium sized companies still have to prepare full statutory accounts, however, for approval by their shareholders.

The value of being classed as a small or medium sized company is that these are allowed certain **filing exemptions** with the registrar of companies. The accounts they lodge, and which will be available for public inspection, need not contain all the information that has to be disclosed by large companies. As a result, the small or medium sized company contains the competitive advantage of not having to disclose so much financial information to its competitors.

The principle of **economies of scale** suggests that smaller firms should be driven out of the market as a result of their higher unit costs. Other common competitive weaknesses include:

- **reliance on a single product** for survival
- a relative **lack of business expertise**
- limited **financial resources** to withstand competition or economic downturn, and to employ specialists.

The survival of the small firm

AQA	M6
EDEXCEL	M6
OCR	M4
WJEC	M10
CCEA	M4

There are a number of reasons why small firms continue to survive.

- **Supplying a local or limited market:**
  - supplying personal services such as hairdressing and plumbing
  - operating in a particular segment of the market, e.g. domestic building extensions and improvements
  - providing convenience (the 'corner shop')
  - concentrating on specialist or luxury items with limited demand, such as specialist firms for coin and stamp collectors
  - working in areas where growth is naturally limited, like the markets for personal services.
- **The policy of the owners:**
  - a lack of ambition
  - the desire to remain in charge
  - the wish to avoid risk.
- **Vertical disintegration:**
  - where larger companies sub-contract out to small firms, because they find it unprofitable to do the work themselves.

Key points from AS

- **Economies of scale**
  Revise AS pages 56–57

- **The attraction of entrepreneurship:**
  - some small firms are established by people wanting to work for themselves
  - they give those who dislike working for a large organisation the chance to work for themselves.

> Two related factors are the increasing popularity of franchise operations, and the growth in the number of self-employed people.

Small firms also have a number of typical strengths that help them to survive. They are often **quicker to respond** to market forces, their **communication** between management and staff is normally more efficient, and **labour relations** are usually good.

Encouraging the survival

The growth of the small-firms sector has been encouraged by government policies in the 1990s, in an attempt to stimulate the economy, and encourage entrepreneurism and employment. The government has tried to support this through policies attempting to:

- **reduce bureaucracy** – cutting the statistical and other information required by government authorities
- **provide a more helpful taxation policy** – e.g. by lowering corporation tax levels for small firms, and establishing a turnover threshold for VAT registration
- **provide assistance** – e.g. through various DTI initiatives such as
  - the **Small Business Service**, dedicated to helping small firms and to representing their interests across government
  - local business centres – **Business Links** (England), **Business Shops** (Scotland), **Business Connect** offices (Wales) and **EDnet** business advice centres (Northern Ireland)
  - the **New Deal** initiative
  - the **Phoenix Fund**, which encourages entrepreneurship in disadvantaged communities
  - the **Small Firms Loan Guarantee Scheme**, which guarantees loans for small businesses that have tried and failed to obtain a loan due to a lack of security
  - supporting EU schemes for small and medium sized firms, e.g. the EU's **European Structural Funds**.

	1991 *£ billion*	*1997* *£ billion*
Agricultural guidance	1.5	2.2
Regional policy	4.5	7.7
Social policy	3.0	4.4

Figure 2.2 *Expenditure on EU Structural Funds*   *Source: European Commission*

> Profit maximisation is a less important business objective for many small-scale entrepreneurs who are often more concerned to stay **independent**.

Progress check

1 What competitive weaknesses do small firms often have?

1 No economies of scale; reliance on a single product; limited expertise; limited resources.

2.3 Multinationals

After studying this section you should be able to:

- describe the benefits from operating as a multinational company
- compare the benefits and drawbacks to the host country as a result of multinationals operating there

The importance of multinationals

AQA	M6
EDEXCEL	M6
OCR	M4
WJEC	M10
CCEA	M4

Key points from AS

- **Limited companies**
  Revise AS pages 37–38

A multinational company operates internationally, although its ownership is based in a single country. The ownership may be in the form of a **holding company**, which 'holds' (controls) the different subsidiaries. Many of the UK's best-known companies are multinationals.

Analysis by region	Turnover		Operating profit	
	£ m	%	£ m	%
Europe	952.2	29	170.9	35
Americas	1006.2	30	104.8	22
Africa	386.7	12	61.0	13
Asia/Pacific	966.5	29	143.2	30
	3311.6	100	479.9	100

Figure 2.3 *International performance, BOC group.*   Source: The BOC Group plc report and accounts 1999

Multinationals contribute over one-third of total world production, and the larger multinationals generate output and turnover levels that exceed the GDP of many countries. As a result, many governments offer a range of (financial) incentives to encourage multinationals to base their operations in the countries concerned.

- ● BP Amoco activity (former BP)
- ● BP Amoco activity (former Amoco)

Figure 2.4 *World-wide involvement of BP Amoco following the merger*

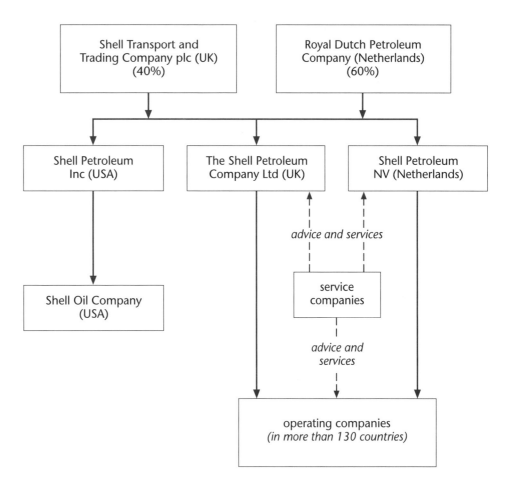

Figure 2.5 *The structure of a multinational*   Source: Royal Dutch/Shell Group of Companies

Multinationals have grown in number and importance because they gain from the following benefits.

Some analysts have suggested that the labour-cost element of a sports or fashion shoe retailing at £50 can be less than 10p.

- **Cheaper labour or materials found in different countries**. General Motors relocated production from the USA to Mexico; footwear/sportswear multinationals such as Nike also gain labour-cost benefits from manufacturing in the Far East.
- **Entering tariff-protected markets**. One way round the EU's Common External Tariff is to set up production in one of its countries. Overseas multinationals like Nissan, Toyota, Epson, Tatung and Ricoh have located in the UK and now form part of the 'home' economy.
- **Avoiding regulation in the home country**. Legislation and other restrictions (e.g. through the Competition Commission in the UK) can be avoided by the multinational basing some of its operations in a different country.

Benefits of multinationals to the host economy

Advocates of the free market system and 'market forces' argue that multinationals are subject to the same basic laws of supply and demand as any other business. A host economy gains many benefits from allowing multinationals to operate.

- **Unemployment is reduced**. Multinationals are major employers of labour, and can help reduce regional unemployment (e.g. Nissan locating in north-east England, badly hit by the decline of traditional manufacturing and construction). In addition, support firms such as component manufacturers and suppliers of canteen and cleaning services grow in the local area and provide further employment.
- **Other factors of production are employed more fully**. They will be used more efficiently as a result of competition created by the multinational.
- **Advanced technology is introduced**. Examples in the UK include technology-

based multinationals like Epson (printers), Tatung (televisions) and Toyota (vehicles) bringing ideas and expertise into the UK economy. Training in more advanced techniques and skills may also develop in the local area.

Examples include introduction of Japanese-originated working practices into the UK economy.

- **Modern work practices are introduced.** Many multinationals have work practices that emphasise teamwork, shared goals and employee participation in decision-making. They may also operate no-redundancy policies.
- **There is greater choice and higher income.** Consumers benefit from wider product choice, and the economy gains through the multinational's activities, both at home (employment rises, tax revenue is generated, and greater expertise improves economic competitiveness), and by exporting (balance of payments benefits).
- **Improved infrastructure.** One common side-effect of multinationals setting up in a country is an improvement to the local infrastructure, which is often financed by the multinational itself.

Problems of multinationals to the host economy

The policies and actions of a multinational may not always bring benefits to the country in which it is based. It may cause a number of tensions as a result of the economic power it wields.

Some UK-based multinationals have taken action, arguably as a result of the UK not having joined the Eurozone: examples are on page 23.

- **The multinational concentrates on its own interests** rather than those of the host country:
  - it may decide at short notice to move production out of the country, causing unemployment and other economic problems to the areas affected, and hitting the host country's balance of payments and level of economic growth
  - it can adjust its costs between its various subsidiaries to gain maximum benefits from one country's lower taxation requirements
  - it has the power to move its reserves between different countries, gaining financial advantage but causing currency fluctuations.
- The multinational may also use its economic power in ways that are **socially undesirable.** Accusations of bribery, corruption, financial irregularity and the exploitation of cheap labour have been levelled against some multinationals, and raw materials may be obtained with only limited regard for the environmental impact or long-term stability and growth of the countries concerned.

> The importance of multinationals lies in their significant economic contribution to a country's economy.
>
> **KEY POINTS**

Progress check

1 What are the (a) benefits and (b) problems presented to the host country as a result of multinational operations?

1 a) Reduced unemployment; efficient use of factors of production; introduction of advanced technology and modern work practices; overall increase in consumer choice and income. (b) Likely concentration on the multinational's interests and not those of the host country; possible socially undesirable environmental and other practices.

Sample question and model answer

1

Tom and Tricia have been good friends for many years. In 1997 they became equal partners in a publishing firm. They thought carefully about the type of business structure which they should have, discussing issues such as unlimited liability and continuity of existence and the fact that a partnership is not a body corporate. They are now considering whether they should take on a sleeping partner or a full partner. As owners of the business, **they** are able to make the decision which best suits them.

(a) Outline the meaning of the following terms:
    (i) 'unlimited liability'   [2]
    (ii) 'continuity of existence'   [2]
    (iii) 'body corporate'   [2]
    (iv) 'sleeping partner'.   [2]

(b) Examine why a business partnership, such as that between Tom and Tricia, may prefer to take on a 'sleeping partner' rather than a full partner.   [10]

(c) To what extent does the form of business ownership determine who takes the decisions in a private sector business?   [12]

CCEA 1999, GCE A Level, Business Studies, Paper 1

Acceptable definitions, though for (i) explain that the partners only have to pay business debts if the partnership's net assets are not sufficient.

(a) (i) If Tom and Tricia's business fails, they will have to find money from their own wealth to pay the business debts.

(ii) When there is a change in the people who own the business (e.g. Tom or Tricia leave), a business such as a limited company continues automatically, but there is no continuity for a partnership or sole trader.

(iii) This is a business that exists in its own right such as a limited company, not a partnership.

(iv) This partner gives finance to the partnership, but takes no part in daily decision-making.

This is a rather limited answer, which adds little to the point made in (a) (iv). Points need to be made that a sleeping partner may not be a suitable full partner due to lack of business knowledge, or inability/unwillingness to get on with Tom and Tricia (partnership disputes may be more likely with three partners). A third partner could also bind Tom and Tricia with his/her decisions made on behalf of the partnership.

(b) If Tom and Tricia decide to take on a sleeping partner, they have the advantage of getting someone who will help to finance their business, but who will not interfere with their decision-making.

Accurate points. Mention could be made of two other important forms of private sector business: (a) the franchisee takes basic business decisions but has to follow the franchisor's strategic policy (e.g. on layout, decor, advertising, etc.); (b) decisions in a co-operative are taken by the members who own it, each member having a single vote.

(c) In a sole trader business, all decisions are taken by the single owner. There is nothing to stop the sole trader involving any staff in the decisions, but it is the sole trader's responsibility only. With a partnership, decisions could be on the basis of a majority vote unless it is a decision to do with any change in the nature of a partnership. Again the partners can involve staff in decision-making if they choose to do so. A private limited company's strategic decisions are carried out by the Board, who will delegate day-to-day decision-making to managers. Although the company is owned by shareholders, some of them may not be directors or otherwise work in the company, although they can attend shareholder meetings and take part in any votes. The public limited company will have more shareholders, who help take major decisions at shareholder meetings (e.g. Annual General Meetings and Extraordinary General Meetings). Again there will be directors who are involved in the more strategic decision-making, with delegation of the more tactical decisions to their managers.

Practice examination question

1

> **Arthur uses his loaf**
>
> Arthur Lee is an unassuming individual who gets on with his work quietly and efficiently. Arthur owns a small bakery firm, "Lee's Loaves", which he runs on his own. "My type of business they call a sole trader," Arthur says, "but if 'sole' means being on your own, that's a strange name to use since I'm hardly ever on my own here."
>
> In fact, Arthur employs three full-time staff in the bakery, and two full-time as well as three part-time Saturday employees in his shop. Arthur admits, "It's a difficult one when you're talking to people, to try to explain the size of your business: you say 'sole proprietor', and they think you're doing it all yourself."
>
> Arthur explained "They say I'm part of what they call the 'small firm sector', but my firm is big enough for me. In fact, it's been growing since before last Christmas. What we found in November was an increase in demand, which continued up to and beyond Christmas. I had to hire an extra couple of part-timers to help out on Saturday, and we're still doing so well that I'm pleased to say we could keep them on."
>
> Arthur is one of the local success stories, but he admits that there are some areas of the business he leaves well alone. "Although I'm happy enough to do a lot of the administration myself, my background is one of baking bread and cooking cakes. I leave the specialist accounts work to my accountant, who comes in every Friday. And before you ask, the answer's no – he doesn't 'cook the books'!"

(a) "Lee's Loaves" operates as a sole trader. Why might a firm such as "Lee's Loaves" give a false impression if it uses 'number of employees' as the only indicator of its size? [8]

(b) Sole traders make up the majority of businesses in the United Kingdom, and dominate the 'small-firm sector'. Explain why a healthy small-firm sector is so important to the UK economy. [8]

Chapter 3

Business objectives

The following topics are covered in this chapter:

- *Strategic planning*
- *Strategic analysis*

- *Decision tree analysis*

3.1 Strategic planning

After studying this section you should be able to:

- *describe how organisations view the meaning of 'strategy'*
- *explain the purpose of, and influences on, mission statements*
- *show how SWOT and STEP analysis relate to strategic planning*

LEARNING SUMMARY

'Strategy'

AQA	M6
EDEXCEL	M6
OCR	M10
WJEC	M5
CCEA	M4

Henry Mintzberg has suggested that different organisations use 'strategy' to mean different things. It can be one of five Ps:

- a **plan** – for finance, human resources, etc.
- a **ploy** – a short-term strategy with very limited objectives
- a **pattern of behaviour** – where managers consistently act the same way (e.g. buying patterns, pricing behaviour)
- a **position** in respect to others – how the firm obtains and then defends its position in the market (e.g. using its reputation for safety or good service)
- a **perspective** – the core beliefs of the people running the organisation.

Professor Chandler of Harvard Business School defined 'strategy' as:

'the determination of the basic long-term goals and objectives of an enterprise, and the adoption of courses of action and the allocation of resources necessary for carrying out these goals'.

The key features of business strategy are therefore:

- **determining long-term goals**
- **adopting courses of action**
- **allocating resources.**

Mission statements

Mission statements are influenced by the organisation's culture and structure, the nature of its competition and markets, and the beliefs and attitudes of its owners.

The organisation will set **objectives** in order to achieve long-term strategic plans. The objective that embraces all others is its **mission statement**. The purpose of the mission statement is to:

- **communicate** the objectives and values of the organisation
- **influence** employee behaviour and attitudes, and
- help in achieving **congruence** ('harmony' or 'balance' in the organisation).

Key points from AS

- **Goals and objectives**
  Revise AS page 35
- **Stakeholders**
  Revise AS page 42

Pilkington plc's mission statement

'Our mission is to be a dynamic, market-driven, global provider of glass products, judged best-in-class by our customers, our people and our shareholders.'

Mission statements – and business objectives generally – will be influenced by the organisation's **stakeholders**. According to Mendelow's model (1991), stakeholders can be rated as a result of their:

The board of directors illustrates stakeholders with both high power (through their control of the company) and high interest (e.g. through share ownership)

- **power** – i.e. their **ability** to influence the organisation
- **interest** – i.e. their **willingness** to influence the organisation (which depends on their degree of interest in it).

Stakeholder power × stakeholder interest = stakeholder influence

A stakeholder with high power and high interest will be more influential than one with low power and/or low interest.

Planning

AQA	M6
EDEXCEL	M5, M6
OCR	M10
WJEC	M5
CCEA	M4

In carrying out its strategic planning, managers will conduct both an **internal audit** and an **external audit** for the organisation. The overall audit is often built around a **SWOT** analysis (page 63), with the external audit having a **STEP** focus (page 71).

Key points from AS

- **SWOT analysis**
  Revise AS page 109

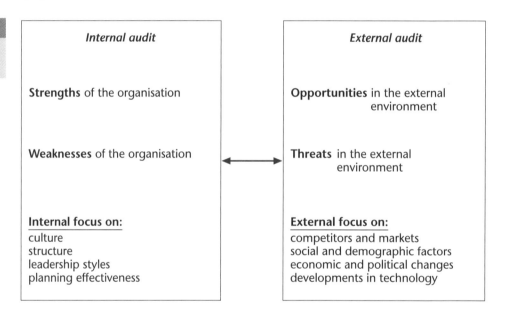

Internal audit	External audit
Strengths of the organisation	**Opportunities** in the external environment
Weaknesses of the organisation	**Threats** in the external environment
Internal focus on: culture structure leadership styles planning effectiveness	**External focus on:** competitors and markets social and demographic factors economic and political changes developments in technology

KEY POINTS

Other influences on strategic planning include Ansoff's matrix (page 63), investment appraisal (page 91) and the use of decision trees (page 46).

Progress check

1 List Mintzberg's 'five Ps'.
2 What are the purposes of mission statements?

1 Plan; ploy; pattern of behaviour; position; perspective.
2 To communicate objectives; to influence employee behaviour; to help achieve congruence.

3.2 Strategic analysis

After studying this section you should be able to:

- describe and evaluate the relevance of Porter's matrix and his five-point framework
- explain the strengths and weaknesses of benchmarking
- outline the value of contingency planning

Strategy and the environment

AQA	M6
EDEXCEL	M5, M6
OCR	M10
WJEC	M1, M5
CCEA	M4

> 'Value added' is the difference in the financial value of the output (the finished product) compared with the financial value of its inputs.

Porter's matrix

Professor Michael Porter of the Harvard Business School developed a **generic strategy** framework, in which he argues that competitive advantage results from selecting the generic strategy that best fits the organisation's competitive environment. Once this is done, **value-adding activities** can be organised to support the chosen strategy.

He identifies three main options for a firm:

- **cost leadership** – being the lowest cost producer of a product
- **differentiation** – creating consumer perception that the product is 'better' than those of competitors
- **focus** – concentrating on either cost leadership or differentiation in markets/segments.

According to this analysis the entrepreneur must decide whether to try to sell differentiated products at premium prices or whether to produce at a lower cost than competitors, and also whether to target the whole market or concentrate on a niche or segment. Porter's framework (or matrix) summarises the two key strategic decisions.

- Should the **scope** of the organisation's strategy be broad or narrow?
- Should this strategy **focus** on cost leadership or on differentiation?

Figure 3.1 *Porter's generic strategy matrix*   *Source: adapted from Porter, 1985*

Key points from AS

- **Benchmarking**
  Revise AS pages 128–29

> It is argued that many Japanese car manufacturers have successfully adopted this hybrid approach.

Porter argues that the best competitive situation is to be based on one of the four segments.

Limitations to his framework have been suggested.

- Businesses can succeed by adopting a **'hybrid'** strategy, which combines elements of differentiation with cost- and price-competitiveness.
- Cost leadership does not guarantee product sales – buying decisions are often made on the basis of the product rather than the price.

Analysing the competitive environment

Porter also (1980) developed a five-point framework for analysing the nature and extent of competition within an industry. He suggests there are five competitive forces a firm can analyse to determine the extent of its competition.

- The threat of **new entrants** to the industry – this will vary according to these barriers to entry:
  - the capital investment required
  - the degree of brand loyalty from the market's consumers
  - economies of scale available
  - the amount of resistance from existing firms in the industry.
- The threat of **substitute products** – influences here are the degree to which the substitute product's features (its price, performance, etc.) match those in the industry, and how willing consumers are to switch to the substitute.
- The power of **buyers or customers** – this depends on their number (and on the number of firms), and the costs they face in switching to substitutes.
- The power of **suppliers** – for example, the number and size of firms in the market, and the degree of brand loyalty customers have to these firms' products.
- **Rivalry** among firms in the industry – e.g. the level of price competition and non-price competition.

> It is important to repeat this 'five-forces' analysis because of changes occurring in the industry. Doing so will help the firm gain a competitive advantage over others.
>
> **KEY POINTS**

Benchmarking

AQA	M6
EDEXCEL	M5, M6
OCR	M10
WJEC	M5
CCEA	M4

The benchmarking process seeks out 'best practice' from other organisations, compares these practices with the firm's own practice, and therefore leads to an improvement in the firm's practice. It may be based on a simple **comparative analysis**, but is often seen as a much wider **performance improvement tool** of the firm.

A typical benchmarking process

- Identify the subject for benchmarking
- Examine own procedures
- Select the elements to be benchmarked
- Identify a benchmarking organisation
- Collect data on the organisation
- Undertake a comparative analysis of the data
- Compare results
- Plan changes to the elements/procedures

Most benchmarking is **external**, but it can also be carried out **internally**, e.g. where a multinational has a number of similar units and operations.

Strengths and weaknesses of benchmarking

A 1995 study by the CBI in conjunction with Coopers and Lybrand suggests these benefits.

- More meaningful and realistic targets are set.
- There is early warning of competitive disadvantage.
- Staff motivation increases by involvement in benchmarking and through team-working.

Key points from AS

- **Benchmarking**
  Revise AS pages 128–29

The limitations of benchmarking include the difficulty in selecting performance measures and the most appropriate benchmark 'partner', and an inability to obtain suitable benchmark data.

Contingency planning

AQA	M6
EDEXCEL	M5, M6
OCR	M10
WJEC	M5
CCEA	M4

A recent illustration of universal contingency planning was the 'millennium bug', which (it was feared) would affect computers throughout the world by their inability to recognise the year 2000 as a date.

An important part of planning and strategic analysis is to ask **'what if?'** questions. **Contingency planning** encourages managers to consider alternative courses of action if some emergency or unforeseen event occurred. Examples of such crises include environmental disasters, selling dangerous products or contaminated foodstuffs, and the collapse of a major customer/market.

Each or all of the organisation's major functions – marketing, human resources, finance, production, buying, etc. – may be affected by the crisis. Staff from each function should therefore be involved in contingency planning. This has the advantage of improving motivation through involvement, but illustrates the fact that this form of planning can be expensive.

If an organisation's management recognises the value of contingency planning, the normal procedure for contingency planning is to:

- outline and examine all possible **crisis scenarios**
- **plan** for each crisis
- **test the plan**, e.g. by running a computer simulation.

If a crisis does occur, the organisation's public relations department is likely to play a major part in managing the crisis.

Progress check

1 What **three** options are identified in Porter's matrix analysis?

2 State the five points in Porter's competitive environment framework.

2 Threat of new entrants; threat of substitute products; power of buyers/customers; power of suppliers; rivalry in the industry.

1 Cost leadership; differentiation; focus.

3.3 Decision tree analysis

After studying this section you should be able to:

- *explain the purpose of decision tree analysis*
- *construct a decision tree*
- *evaluate the strengths and weaknesses of this form of analysis*

The purpose of decision trees

AQA	M6
EDEXCEL	M4
OCR	M10
WJEC	M5
CCEA	M4

Decision trees are therefore similar to some forms of **investment appraisal** (page 91), although decision tree analysis takes greater account of the element of uncertainty.

These are tree-like diagrams representing business situations, where a series of decisions need to be made. Each decision has its own 'branch' on the tree, the branch leading to further branches that represent the outcomes of the decision. The tree shows all possible outcomes (alternative courses of action) that can be taken under all conditions.

Each possible outcome is given:

- an estimated **monetary value**
- an estimated **probability** of it happening.

These values, **weighted** by their probabilities, are then calculated as **expected values**. The decision-taker will select the line of action that results in the **highest expected value** (the '**expectation**').

Constructing the decision tree

Here is a question with a step-by-step construction of a decision tree.

> In the summer, Laura runs an ice cream van. She finds that traffic congestion occasionally causes her delays and affects her sales, but she has the option of changing route to avoid the delay. Laura knows that cold weather affects her sales.
>
> Laura now has the chance to rent a small kiosk in her local town centre where she can sell her ice cream. She knows that sales from the kiosk will also be affected by cold weather. Laura cannot run the kiosk and continue with her ice cream van. Should she rent the kiosk?

1 Start with the main decision

Laura's first decision – ice cream van or kiosk? – is recorded ('D1').

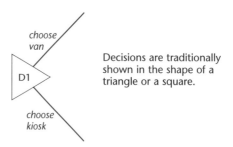

Decisions are traditionally shown in the shape of a triangle or a square.

2 Construct event circles

Alternatives extending from these circles are now shown (and £ values are also recorded later in these circles).

Laura faces two alternatives with the van. First, whether there will be a traffic delay or not (event circle E1). If there is no delay (E3), the second alternative – warm or cold weather – can be plotted. If there is a delay, however, Laura has a second decision to make (D2): this branch is developed later.

The only alternative Laura faces with the kiosk (E2) relates to the weather, and so this can be plotted.

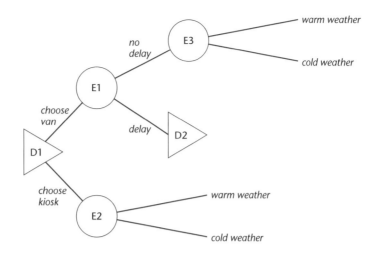

If there is a traffic delay, Laura must make her second decision: change the route or stay on the same route? This decision is plotted: the resulting event circles (E4 and E5) are then given the alternatives of warm and cold weather.

The range of alternatives for Laura with her ice cream van is therefore:

- no delay, with either warm weather or cold weather
- delay but stay on same route, with warm weather or cold weather
- delay and change route, with either warm or cold weather.

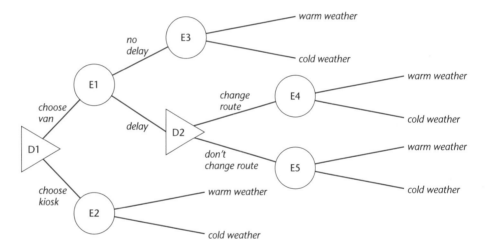

3 Record the probabilities

Laura believes that, on any day, there is a 75% chance of it being warm. She also thinks the probability of being delayed in the van on any one day is 30%.

The weather probabilities (0.75 and 0.25) and the chance of traffic delay (0.70 and 0.30) are recorded.

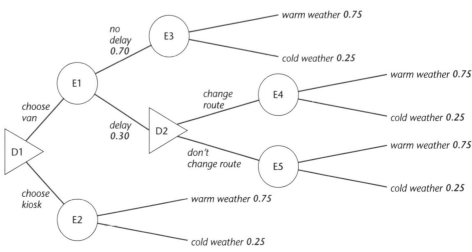

4 Plot the values and calculate the results – the expected values (EVs)

Laura's estimated daily sales are:

		£
Warm days	van, without experiencing any delays	140
	van, with delays and a change of route	110
	van, with delays and not changing route	100
	kiosk	125
Cold days	van, without experiencing any delays	90
	van, with delays and a change of route	75
	van, with delays and not changing route	65
	kiosk	80

Working from the right, the financial values are plotted, and multiplied by the probability score.

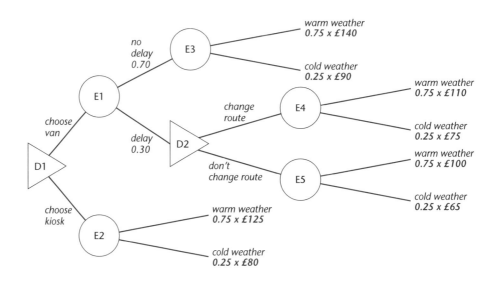

Kiosk calculation:

EV for E2 = (0.75 × £125) £93.75 + (0.25 × £80) £20 = £113.75

Van calculations:

EV for E3 (no delay) = (0.75 × £140) £105 + (0.25 × £90) £22.50 = £127.50

EV for E4 (delay, change route) =
(0.75 × £110) £82.50 + (0.25 × £75) £18.75 = £101.25

EV for E5 (delay, no change) =
(0.75 × £100) £75 + (0.25 × £65) £16.25 = £91.25

D2 (change route or not) calculations show that Laura would decide to change the route, because of the higher sales income. This figure is therefore used to calculate E1.

E1 = (E3 £127.50 × 0.7) + (E4 £101.25 × 0.3) = £89.25 + £30.38 = £119.63

5 Show the calculation results in the decision tree, and make the decision

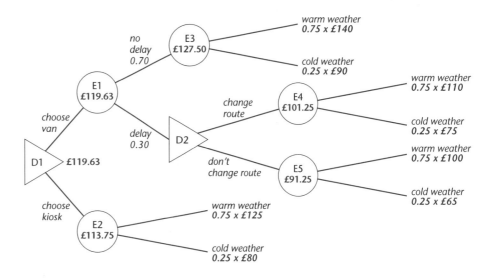

The calculations show that Laura should continue operating her ice cream van: the 'choose van' option is worth £119.63 sales, whereas the 'choose kiosk' option is worth only £113.75 sales.

The value of decision trees

Decision trees are suited to situations where there is a **logical sequence of events** or alternatives that are followed in **conditions of uncertainty**. They are most effective where a **similar past event** (e.g. launch of a product) provides quantitative information that can give **realistic estimates** for the new situation.

> Examples of suitable use include decisions on whether to buy or hire equipment, develop and sell a new product, or build a new factory.

Decision tree analysis requires management to:

- allocate probabilities to events occurring, which makes them think logically and in quantitative terms
- set out these events in a logical manner, which assists their planning
- consider the expected costs of failure as well as of success.

The limitations of decision tree analysis are that:

- it cannot take full account of the uncertainty of business
- the information on which the tree is based will be incomplete or inaccurate
- it ignores qualitative aspects of the decision.

As a result, the tree gives an inaccurate and incomplete overall picture.

> Constructing a decision tree encourages a full and logical analysis of a problem, covering all eventualities, before undertaking a project.

KEY POINTS

Progress check

1 List the steps in constructing a decision tree.

Sample question and model answer

1

Maypole Manufacturing Ltd is planning a major project and has a number of decisions it must make. Stella, the project manager, has drawn up a decision tree to illustrate the situation. This decision tree is shown in the diagram below.

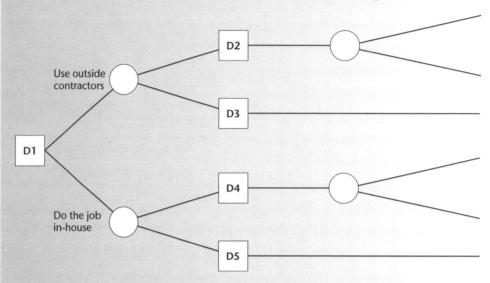

Stella knows that the first major decision is whether to use specialist outside contractors or do the job in-house.

The probability of the project being a success is estimated at 80% if Maypole Manufacturing Ltd uses the more expensive outside contractors. The estimated chance of success if it is done by the less expensive in-house method is 70%.

Failure, using an outside contractor, would cost the firm an estimated £3m. An in-house failure would cost an estimated £2m. If the project fails, whether carried out in-house or by an outside contractor, the firm has decided it will carry out an investigation into the reasons for the failure.

If the project is successful, Maypole Manufacturing Ltd will decide to take on a second similar project using the same method as for the first contract. The chances of success would be 90% if the outside contractors do the work and 85% if it is done in-house.

Two successful projects undertaken by the outside contractors would bring Maypole Manufacturing Ltd an estimated profit of £8m, having paid the contractors for the work. Two successful projects undertaken in-house would bring Maypole Manufacturing Ltd an estimated profit of £9m, having accounted for their own costs.

If the second project fails, even though the first has been a success, it will cost the firm an estimated £1m if the projects are undertaken by the outside contractor and £0.5m if the projects are undertaken in-house.

(i) Draw out and complete the decision tree in the diagram, indicating all probabilities and financial outcomes. (Do not round up any of your answers – keep the full number of decimal places in each calculation.) [10]

(ii) Using only the completed decision tree from your answer to (i) above, state whether Stella should decide to use outside contractors or do the projects in-house. Give a reason for your answer. [2]

(iii) Evaluate the effectiveness of decision tree analysis in planning. Illustrate your answer with the example of Maypole Manufacturing Ltd. [18]

CCEA 2000, GCE A Level, Business Studies, Paper 1

Sample question and model answer *(continued)*

(i)

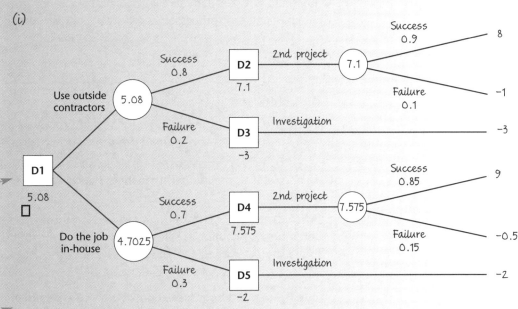

This is an accurate answer: the results and descriptions are clearly shown.

Again, an accurate statement: it is important to state this is a statement of the 'financial outcome' rather than the cost.

The answer could also explain that one of the strengths of using decision trees is that they display the calculations visually in a clear and summarised way.

A good answer: a more detailed one would be given by separating probabilities and financial estimates into two discussion points, and providing more illustrations (e.g. examples of changing external environments, such as competitor and government actions).

(ii) Stella should use outside contractors, because the expected financial outcome is ₤5 080 000 rather than ₤4 702 500 if she were to do it in-house.

(iii) A decision tree provides financial information for managers. In this case, it helps Stella decide whether she goes to an outside contractor or not. Stella will have consulted other managers and staff to get the various probabilities, which illustrates that decision trees make people undertake a lot of research. The results of this research must be converted to financial figures, which is another value of using decision trees.

Limitations of decision trees are that the figures and probabilities used are only guesswork, being based on estimates. Here, the staff at Maypole Manufacturing may be using inaccurate or incomplete information to base these calculations on: for example, the costs of failure are only estimated, and could be much greater in reality. Maypole is also going to be affected by changes in the external environment, which can make the decision tree analysis become out-of-date.

Practice examination question

1 O'Brien Ltd is a company in the food processing industry. It is a market leader in the manufacture of processed dairy products such as cheese and yoghurt.

At a recent board meeting, the directors discussed the contents of this article (extract below).

Difficulties at Depps

Depps Ltd, one of the leading suppliers of processed foodstuffs, was today found guilty of supplying contaminated products to Britain's leading supermarkets…

… At the press conference, the managing director for Depps Ltd, Jules Binoche, apologised but maintained that there had never been any danger to public health.

When asked how Depps Ltd would recover from this setback, he stated 'Our contingency planning is robust, and we remain confident that we shall soon re-establish ourselves as a leading player in the market-place…'

At the O'Brien Ltd board meeting, there was substantial discussion concerning the nature and value of contingency planning. The Production Director commented 'In some ways, this Depps business will be a boost to us, and we have spare productive capacity if necessary. However, in the light of this food contamination problem faced by Depps, we need to review our own contingency planning. I'm concerned that our plans don't consider such an eventuality in sufficient detail.'

The Sales Director replied 'There's hardly any need to panic, given our excellent track record in food production. Where's the problem? The bottom line for me is that, whilst it's all very well to talk about reviewing, developing and improving our own contingency planning, this contingency planning business is very expensive, and there's no guarantee that it will work. Why bother?'

(a) What is 'contingency planning'? [4]

(b) If '… this contingency planning business is very expensive, and there's no guarantee that it will work…', why do companies like O'Brien Ltd commit resources to it? [8]

Chapter 4

Corporate culture

The following topics are covered in this chapter:

- *Corporate culture*
- *Coping with change*

4.1 Corporate culture

After studying this section you should be able to:

- *examine the influence of management style on an organisation*
- *explain how change should be managed in an organisation*

LEARNING SUMMARY

Management style

AQA	M6
EDEXCEL	M6
OCR	M10
WJEC	M1
CCEA	M4

Theorists such as Herzberg and Maslow focus on people's **needs**, rather than the job they are doing, by focusing on the **social environment** of the organisation. Managers have four traditional functions, which are carried out within a framework of **management style** and **organisational culture**:

- planning
- controlling
- directing
- organising.

Types of management style

> Typical examples include many small firms, where the emphasis is on communication and employee involvement.

The **democratic** manager guides and advises, but allows the group or individual to make decisions. This style is more closely associated with the **human relations** theorists, notably McGregor's Theory Y approach. It is found in organisations that have:

- efficient and **open communication** procedures
- **limited chains of command**
- **routine delegation**.

The **autocratic** manager might allow some individual and group involvement, but makes the final decision. Concentrating decisions in the hands of senior management encourages a 'top-down', centralised structure influenced more by the work of **classical theorists** (such as Taylor). Traditionally, examples include state-operated services such as the police and armed forces.

> The *laissez-faire* approach can be criticised if the manager avoids the functions of controlling and directing.

The **laissez-faire** ('let it be') manager chooses not to interfere in the work of the group. This style of management can operate successfully if the firm has cohesive groups prepared to work together to achieve common objectives.

Another way to analyse management styles is to identify extreme situations. For example, an organisation's management might be seen in terms of the dimensions set out on page 54.

> **Key points from AS**
>
> - **Motivation**
>   *Revise AS pages 101–103*

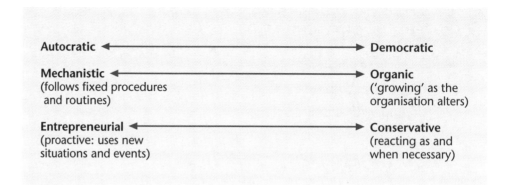

Autocratic ◄─────────────────────► Democratic

Mechanistic ◄─────────────────────► Organic
(follows fixed procedures   ('growing' as the
 and routines)   organisation alters)

Entrepreneurial ◄─────────────────────► Conservative
(proactive: uses new   (reacting as and
situations and events)   when necessary)

Influences on management style include **personal preferences**, the amount of **training** in and the level of **awareness** of the different styles, the nature of the **tasks** being managed, the pace of **change** and the organisation's **culture**.

Organisational culture

AQA	M6
EDEXCEL	M6
OCR	M10
WJEC	M1
CCEA	M4

A 'culture' is created from various beliefs, ideals, norms and values. Each organisation has a culture, in much the same way that we may represent different cultures. Its culture is expressed in the **actions of the people** who make up the organisation. It is also seen in the organisation's **rules**, **procedures**, **structures** and **systems**.

Culture is important to an organisation, because it influences all of the organisation's activities. It has a particular influence on employee **motivation** (and therefore output, quality and productivity), the **image/appeal of the organisation** (e.g. as an employer), its degree of **creativity** as an organisation, and the nature and quality of **industrial relations**.

Types of organisational culture

Theorists such as **R. Harrison** and **C. Handy** suggest these organisational cultures exist.

Four distinct organisational cultures are said to exist.

Culture	Features	Advantage	Disadvantage
Power culture	mainly associated with small entrepreneurial organisations relies on a central source of power delegating to a surrounding 'web'	few layers in the hierarchy, with wide spans of control	control remains centralised at the top
Role culture	exists in organisations structured by function and specialism consists of chains of command and lines of authority	roles, status and positions are known	relies heavily on rules and procedures
Task culture	associated with matrix and project-based structures decentralised and flexible (team-based) organisations	effective where flexibility and teamwork are important	control may be difficult
Person culture	typical of small professional organisations clusters of people operate in a minimal structure	creativity is encouraged, with a quick response time	can be difficult to set targets and monitor achievement

Key points from AS

- **Motivation**
  Revise AS pages 101–103

Organisational cultures can also be classified as:

- **hierarchical** cultures, based on the formal hierarchy and chain of command, often having a 'mistake-free' philosophy
- **growth** cultures, associated with matrix- or product-based organisations that encourage a market-based approach, or
- **goal-oriented** cultures, where goals are followed 'at all costs'.

Determinants of an organisation's culture

In addition to management style, other influences on the culture adopted by an organisation include:

- the personal philosophy of its creators
- the type of industry in which it is based
- its degree of dependence on capital/technology or on people
- its geographical location
- its structure ('tall' or 'flat').

Culture and conflict

An organisation's culture helps determine the degree of resistance there will be to change.

A culture that is **unsuitable** for a firm and its employees – e.g. where a merger or privatisation has led to changes in the culture – will result in **low levels of motivation**, and potential **conflict** between management and workforce. The work of McGregor highlights the potential problems when a group of employees has one set of beliefs or expectations, and managers have a different set. If employees have Theory X attitudes but their managers expect Theory Y attitudes, the resultant delegation and involvement is likely to produce poor quality output and misdirected effort. Managers who use Theory X approaches with groups wanting to operate on a Theory Y basis will find that output and morale will again be adversely affected.

> When changing the organisation's culture, managers must **communicate** the nature of these changes to staff, and provide adequate **training** so staff can cope with the new systems arising from these changes. **KEY POINTS**

Progress check

1 How is an organisation's culture expressed?
2 Name **four** types of organisational culture.

2 Power; role; task; person.
1 Through its rules, procedures and people.

4.2 Coping with change

After studying this section you should be able to:

- identify a range of causes of change
- suggest why people may resist change
- explain how change management can lead to effective change

LEARNING SUMMARY

The nature of change

AQA	M6
EDEXCEL	M6
OCR	M6, M10
WJEC	M1, M4
CCEA	M4

> Unforeseen change can sometimes be at least partly anticipated, for example as a result of the firm undertaking **contingency planning** (page 45).

All organisations are affected by changes taking place. Three key questions associated with business change are:

- has it been **anticipated** by management?
- if so, has it been **planned** for by management?
- to what extent is it **controllable** by management?

The most difficult form of change to cope with is that which is **unforeseen** and **uncontrollable**. Examples of unforeseeable change include the financial markets, social and demographic trends, legislation and the actions of competitors.

Most causes of change are **external** to the firm, and typically include the following.

New:	Examples
Markets	Eastern European (former communist) countries, e.g. Czech Republic; creation and growth of the mobile telephone market
Legislation	the 1995 Disability Discrimination Act; the 1998 Data Protection Act
Technology	DVDs; environmentally-disposable plastics
Owners	Volkswagen owning Skoda; Wal-Mart taking over Asda
Competition	Football pools and the National Lottery
Tastes	organic foods; clothing fashions

Figure 4.1 illustrates changing tastes in leisure spending. These changes have had a major influence on leisure industry firms such as cinemas and theme parks.

Spending in 1999, £m (% increase since 1989 at current prices)

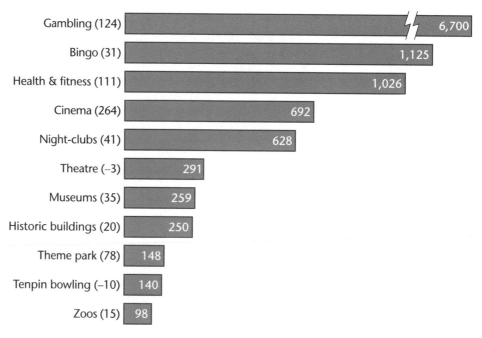

Figure 4.1 Changes in leisure spending from 1989 to 1999

Change also takes place **internally**, e.g. when a firm decides or needs to restructure its operations. The firm may restructure, alter its objectives, if its management style or corporate culture changes. This often occurs when a new chief executive and/or management team is appointed.

Areas of business change can also be analysed under these headings.

Economic	e.g. changing levels of unemployment and skills; balance of payments problems; single European currency
Legislative	e.g. new EU Directives; UK consumer protection laws; human rights legislation
Demographic	e.g. growth in the number of over-65s; fewer young people entering the job market
Technological	e.g. increased computer power; changed production processes
Social	e.g. increasing leisure time; greater awareness of health and fitness

An example of change – particularly as a result of technological and social influences – is in the banking sector of the economy. Figure 4.2 illustrates the continuing trend towards fewer branches, and the changes in cheque transaction volumes. Banks have had to respond to changes in society, e.g. their customers' increased use of credit card transactions at the expense of cheques. They have also introduced change, for example by cost-cutting methods such as reducing the number of branches: the change to greater use of Internet banking is also cheaper for the banks.

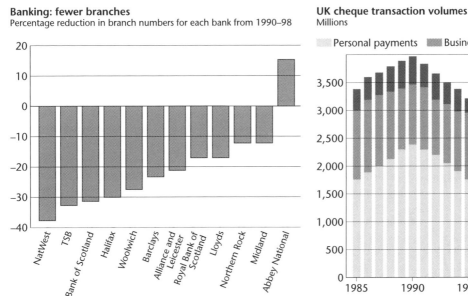

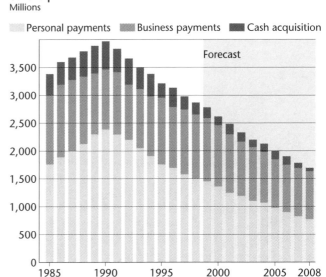

Transactions	Number (millions)		Value (£ billion)	
	1995	**1998**	**1995**	**1998**
Debit cards	1727	2918	65	119
Credit cards	869	1184	40	60

Figure 4.2 Change in the UK banking sector

The pace of change

There are two main categories for the pace of change. These categories are influenced by two factors:

- how **urgent** the need for change is
- what **inertia** there is in the firm's corporate culture – how sluggish or inactive it is.

Step change occurs rapidly: here, the benefit is that the firm responds quickly to change, but the speed can cause disruption and discontent amongst the staff.

Incremental change takes place over a longer period of time, in stages: the change is therefore phased in more gradually, but the relative delay in making changes may cost the firm its competitive advantage.

Managing change

All people – entrepreneurs, managers, employees, suppliers and customers – may resist change for a number of reasons.

- **Personal** reasons:
  - fear of the unknown
  - a low tolerance of change
  - prejudice
  - dislike of the methods being used to implement the change.
- **Communication** reasons:
  - not being given adequate reasons for the change
  - mistrusting or misunderstanding the reasons given.
- **Social** reasons:
  - existing satisfaction with present colleagues, equipment and systems
  - initial dislike of new colleagues, equipment or systems
  - dislike of outside interference.
- **Economic** reasons:
  - lack of belief in ability to acquire the new skills needed
  - an increased fear of unemployment.

> **Kenwood's internal restructuring changes lead to job losses**
>
> 'Since the start of the Kenwood restructuring programme the Group has reduced its workforce by over 40% to 1626.'
>
> *Source: Kenwood annual report 2000*

In 2000, 25% of domestic bank customers were still not prepared to use ATM ('hole in the wall') cash dispenser machines, and 40% stated they would not use the Internet for banking.

Figure 4.3 summarises the requirements for the effective management of change.

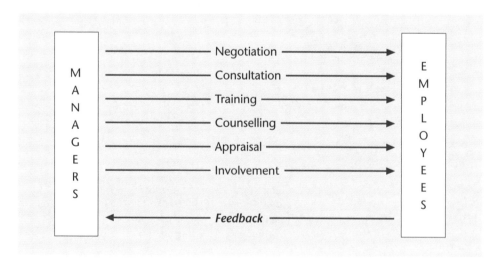

Figure 4.3 Managing change

Managing change involves **planning**, **preparing** for, and **implementing** it. Once the change has been implemented, it will need **evaluating**.

Managers must:

- ensure that full and clear information is given on:
  - reasons for the change
  - method(s) proposed for implementing it
  - likely disruptions to existing work routines
  - progress of the implementation
- give employees their own opportunity to evaluate the possible effects of the proposed changes
- establish working parties, quality circles and training routines for all staff affected by the change
- provide a system to monitor the implementation, which allows employees to give feedback
- continue to monitor the effects of change once the new systems have been fully implemented.

The chances of success

The **leadership style** adopted may affect whether the change is successfully managed. Involvement of staff, e.g. through McGregor's Theory Y approach, should increase motivation levels and ensure communication takes place.

> The greater the level of employee participation and involvement in the process, the more effectively change will be implemented.

KEY POINTS

Progress check

1   State **four** reasons why people may resist change.

1   Personal; economic; communication; social.

Sample question and model answer

1

(a) Explain why some organisations find it difficult to implement change. [10]

(b) To what extent can these difficulties be overcome? [10]

Many relevant points are included, both from the employees' viewpoint and weaknesses in management. We should also consider the organisation itself: e.g. it may be large and bureaucratic, therefore slow to react to change.

(a) Change is difficult to implement in organisations because people resist it for many reasons. There may be personal reasons, such as prejudice against those introducing the change, a fear of the unknown, or just a low tolerance to change. Some people fear that the changes will cause their economic circumstances to alter: for example, the introduction of new technology is often associated with an increased fear of unemployment. Employees may also lack self-belief that they can cope with new equipment or new systems, or may dislike outside interference.

Management may fail in its duty to introduce change through negotiation and consultation. They may not provide adequate reasons for the changes, or may create mistrust in their motives. Their communication procedures may also be at fault, with staff misunderstanding the reasons given for the change. To bring about change, managers sometimes use methods that are disliked by staff content with their existing colleagues and work practices.

The answer concentrates on how these difficulties can be overcome. It should be balanced by explaining that successful implementation of change depends on factors such as the extent to which the change was predicted, whether it is controllable, and the level and quality of the firm's resources (e.g. training schemes etc.).

(b) Managers must seek to ensure staff are consulted and that they (the managers) are also aware of the potential effects of introducing change into the organisation. Before implementing the change, managers should give full information on why and how it is to be implemented, and should give employees the chance to feed ideas back. During the process of change, managers should liaise with staff to monitor progress, and to counsel those staff facing difficulties. A training programme for staff affected by the changes would provide support. Finally, following implementation of the change, all staff should continue to monitor its effects.

Practice examination question

1

> 'The board has established the Management Development and Remuneration Committee (the Committee) which comprises all the non-executive directors of the company...
>
> The Committee's terms of reference are to determine on behalf of the board fair remuneration for the executive directors, which, while set in the context of what the company can reasonably afford, recognises their individual contributions to the company's overall performance. In addition the Committee assists the board in ensuring that the current and future management of the group are recruited, developed and remunerated in appropriate fashion...
>
> The remuneration policy... consists of basic salary... which is in line with the median market salary for each director's responsibilities as advised by independent consultants.'
>
> 'The company's future is embodied in its employees... it is the policy of the group to train and develop employees at all levels so that group objectives can be met... Johnson Matthey recognises the importance of effective employee communications...'
>
> *Source: Extracts from Johnson Matthey plc Annual Report and Accounts, 1999/2000*

In 1999/2000, the five executive directors of Johnson Matthey plc received an average of nearly £375000 each as directors' emoluments (basic salary, plus bonus and benefits). This is a typical level of payment to senior management in a large company.

(a) These and other executive directors receive large incomes. Why is their role vital to the success of firms such as Johnson Matthey plc? [8]

(b) To what extent could a democratic leadership role clash with the existence of large incomes for the top management? [8]

Chapter 5

Marketing

The following topics are covered in this chapter:

- *Analysis, planning and strategy*
- *Market research*
- *New product development*
- *Sales forecasting*

5.1 Analysis, planning and strategy

After studying this section you should be able to:

- *describe the 'marketing concept'*
- *explain the relevance and importance of marketing objectives and strategy*
- *assess the value of Ansoff's matrix in creating a marketing strategy*
- *comment on the nature of the marketing plan and budget*

LEARNING SUMMARY

Marketing objectives

AQA	M4
EDEXCEL	M4
OCR	M4, M5
WJEC	M2
CCEA	M5

The marketing concept

The traditional **production-led** (or **asset-led**) approach to manufacturing concentrated on the product, which would be made using processes that were heavily cost-influenced. As a result, the end products tended to be standardised, the firm placing the product on the market in the hope that it would sell.

Marketing looks at the firm through the eyes of its customers. The basis of the 'marketing concept' is that the customer is seen as the start of the business cycle rather than its end: the firm is **market-led**.

> Marketing objectives often focus on **product differentiation** and **innovation**, and **market growth**.

A market-led approach involves analysing the market, and then making what the market seems to want. It seeks to **differentiate** products on the basis of market requirements, and meet the needs of customers. Production methods and cost-efficient processes remain important, but the emphasis is very much on the **consumer** and the **market**.

Objectives

By focusing on the market, a market-led firm will use marketing objectives as **targets** to achieve. The targets set will be linked to the firm's **mission statement**.

Telewest Communications

'Telewest's vision is to be the chosen provider of multiple broadband services to homes and businesses.'

Source: Telewest plc annual report

Key points from AS

- **Goals and objectives**
  Revise AS page 35
- **Markets and market-led firms**
  Revise AS page 106–107
- **Product differentiation and branding**
  Revise AS pages 112–113

Pilkington plc

'Our mission is to be a dynamic, market-driven, global provider of glass products, judged best-in-class by our customers, our people and our shareholders.'

Source: Pilkington plc annual report

Marketing strategy and planning

AQA	M4
EDEXCEL	M4
OCR	M4, M5
WJEC	M2
CCEA	M5

Competitor actions and government influences are particularly important market influences.

The firm's marketing strategy translates its marketing objectives into action. It is a medium- to long-term approach that balances the marketing and other objectives with the resources available and the practical realities of the market.

The strategy selected will be influenced by:

- **SWOT** results – an evaluation and audit of the firm's (internal) Strengths and Weaknesses, and its (external) Opportunities and Threats
- **market research** data – e.g. on consumer buying behaviour
- past **sales statistics**
- **marketing audits** – reviews of the efficiency of the marketing function
- **resource availability**.

Ansoff's matrix

Igor Ansoff's **product-market framework** is widely used to analyse the strategic direction of a firm. It identifies four options:

- **market penetration** – increasing the firm's market share in its existing markets through its existing products
- **market development** – the firm seeks to enter new markets or segments with its existing products
- **product development** – new products are developed for existing markets
- **diversification** – new products are developed for new markets.

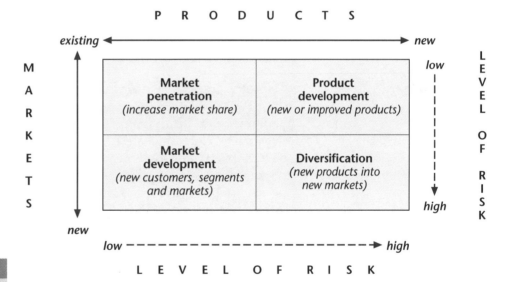

Figure 5.1 Ansoff's matrix

Key points from AS

Goals and objectives
Revise AS page 35

Budgeting
Revise AS pages 84–86

Market segmentation
Revise AS pages 107–108

SWOT analysis
Revise AS page 109

Market penetration

The lowest-risk strategy is to increase market share using existing products within existing markets. **Growth markets** are easier to penetrate than mature or declining ones: to expand in mature and declining ones involves heavy advertising in order to take sales away from competitors.

Market penetration strategy

'The Somerfield Group is already established as the nation's major neighbourhood store and supermarket food retailer. We believe there is ample scope for sustained growth in this market... Our strategy is to address the neighbourhood food retailing opportunity with two strong brands that have distinctive market positions.'

Source: Somerfield plc report and accounts, 1999/2000

Market development

Although the product's strengths and weaknesses are known to the firm, this is a higher-risk strategy, especially since the growth of **globalisation** has led to many firms marketing their existing products in new, international, markets.

Market development

'Our ability to cater to alternative markets was demonstrated by our success at the Bluewater leisure development in Kent, which within four weeks of opening became our busiest restaurant.'

Source: PizzaExpress plc annual report, 1999

Product development

The modern tendency is for products to have **shorter life-cycles**, so product development strategies are widely found. Compared with market development, this strategy brings the advantage that the firm will be dealing with consumers of whom it has some knowledge and experience, and the firm may be able to use existing brand names successfully.

Product development

'...last year, we began our programme of refreshing our brand. The foundations were laid by responding to our customers' desire for more healthy foods, fresh foods, ready meals and organic foods... the lead we have taken in the fast-growing organics market. Over 600 products, which we plan to raise to 1,000 during this year... The range grows ever broader.'

Source: J Sainsbury plc annual report and accounts, 2000

Diversification

This is the highest-risk strategy for a firm. The diversification may be **related** – new products and markets are similar to existing ones – or **unrelated** (growth into products and markets that have little in common with the firm's existing ones).

Diversification

'Sainsbury's Bank opened in February 1997, the first bank to be opened by a British supermarket... Sainsbury's Bank continues to research and launch new products.'

Source: J Sainsbury plc annual report and accounts, 2000

The marketing plan and budget

To implement the strategy, a marketing plan must be drawn up. The plan is important because it **integrates** the various parts of the marketing mix, and it **communicates** the strategy to all staff.

The firm will develop a **promotional strategy**, which will be influenced by the product, its stage in the product life-cycle, and the budget available.

Many promotional strategies are based on **AIDA**. The potential consumer's **Attention** must be captured; **Interest** must be stimulated, followed by a **Desire** for the product, with the **Action** of making a purchase.

The marketing plan needs **resources**, and these are costed in the **marketing budget**, which expresses the marketing plan in financial terms.

As with any budgeting, **variances** can be calculated and compared against actual, allowing **management by exception** to take place.

Some budgets are set by taking last year's budget and adding an increase to account for inflation. Other influences on the budget are:

- the sales forecast
- the **competition** – 'competitor parity' budgeting tries to ensure that the firm's budget is in line with its competitors.

> **KEY POINTS**
>
> The more a firm moves away from its present products and markets, the greater the risk it is taking.

Progress check

1 What are the major influences on how a firm selects its marketing strategy?

2 What are the **four** options in Ansoff's matrix?

2 Market penetration; market development; product development; diversification.

1 SWOT results; market research data; past sales statistics; marketing audits; resource availability.

5.2 Market research

After studying this section you should be able to:

- *distinguish between qualitative and quantitative research*
- *explain the types and relevance of measures of central tendency and dispersion*
- *classify the results of research as controllable or non-controllable*

LEARNING SUMMARY

Types of research

AQA	M4
EDEXCEL	M4
OCR	M4
WJEC	M2
CCEA	M5

• **Opposition**	Who is in the market?	*Competition*
• **Objects**	What do consumers now buy?	*Competitor products*
• **Occupants**	Who are buying these products?	*Consumers*
• **Organisation**	Who is involved in the buying decision?	*Social groups*
• **Objectives**	Why do they buy?	*Buyer behaviour*
• **Occasions**	How frequently do they buy?	*Buyer behaviour*
• **Operations**	How do they buy?	*Distribution channels*

Figure 5.2 *The 'seven Os' of market research*

Market research will generate either **qualitative** or **quantitative** data.

Quantitative research concentrates on **factual** information (e.g. units sold, % share of total market)	**Qualitative research** concentrates on **attitudes** and **opinions** (consumer tastes, likes and dislikes)

To undertake quantitative research a **sample** must be selected as the basis for analysis. The key issues in sampling are the **sampling method** – selecting appropriate people – and the **sample size**, the need to sample an adequate number of people (the larger the sample size, the greater the confidence in the results generated by the sample).

One way to sample is to use the electoral register to pick names at random.

- **Random** sampling is used when a completely representative selection is required. Everyone in the population must have an **equal chance** of being selected.
- **Quota** sampling occurs when the sample is selected on the basis of a **given number**.
- To use a **stratified** sampling approach, the sample is collected on the basis of some **characteristic** in the population (e.g. age or sex).
- **Cluster** sampling is when sampling takes place within a particular **geographical area** only.

Analysing the results

AQA	M4
EDEXCEL	M4
OCR	M4
WJEC	M2
CCEA	M5

'Our own customer satisfaction survey undertaken during April and May... 60% of respondents were between the ages of 25–44... nearly one half of the respondents visited their local PizzaExpress at least once a month but we were also encouraged to find that one fifth were first time users.'

Source: PizzaExpress plc annual report, 1999

Key points from AS

- **Market research**
  Revise AS pages 109–110

Marketing and other managers will need to summarise and describe the **results** of the sample. They may be interested in what is **average**, or **typical**. The data generated by the sample may contain a number of properties that enable managers to determine what is 'average'. Three important properties are:

- **central tendency** – a measure of 'average'
- **dispersion** – a measure of the 'spread' of the data, i.e. how widely dispersed the numbers are
- **skewness** – how symmetrical the raw data are ('skewness' being the term used to describe a lack of symmetry in the raw data).

Measuring central tendency

The **arithmetic mean** is a simple average of the total values of the data, and is calculated by totalling the values and dividing by their number. The **median** is the middle value of an ordered set of data (an **array**). The **mode** is the value occurring most frequently in the data.

> The mode is particularly relevant to retailers, in order to determine the most popular sizes or models sold.

Which measure is used depends on the data and the situation. For example, the mean may give a distorted answer where there is a large fluctuation in sales, due to the extreme values: here, the median may be more appropriate.

- The mean is best used to determine what would result from an **equal distribution** (e.g. consumption per head of a product)
- the median is used when **order or ranking** is important (e.g. the product's sales compared with competitor sales)
- the mode is used to determine the **most commonly occurring** values.

Measure	Advantages	Drawbacks
Mean	• Easy to understand • Uses every value • Can be used for further analysis	• Distorted by extreme values • May give as the answer a value not found in the original data
Median	• Easy to understand • Not influenced by extreme values in the data	• Needs the data to be organised • May be unrepresentative with only a few values
Mode	• Easy to understand • Not influenced by extreme values in the data	• Needs the data to be organised • Cannot be used for further mathematical processing

Measuring dispersion

Measures of location – the mean, median and mode – give an 'average' or 'typical' value. The market researcher or manager may also wish to know how the sample population is **spread**, or dispersed, around the central value.

- The **range** is the difference between the smallest and largest values in the population. It is easy to understand and calculate, useful in providing a quick measure of dispersion, and can be used effectively when there are only a relatively few values in the population. However, it ignores all but two (the largest and smallest) values, and will be affected by an extreme value.
- The **quartile deviation** is often used as the measure of spread when the median is selected as the measure of location. Quartiles divide the data into four equal parts. The **interquartile range** is the difference between the first and third quarters, and the quartile deviation is half of this amount. It therefore concentrates on the **most representative 'middle 50%'** and is therefore not affected by extreme values, although it is more difficult to calculate than the range.

In practice, the standard deviation is easily obtained using a calculator.

- The **standard deviation** is used to measure dispersion when the mean is used for location. It represents the average deviation from the mean and is calculated using the formula:

$$\sigma = \sqrt{\frac{\Sigma(x - \bar{x})^2}{n}}$$

Where σ = the standard deviation $\bar{x}$ = the mean
      Σ = the sum of n = number of values
      x = a value

The standard deviation can be developed further mathematically, but can be distorted by extreme values.

> Selecting the 'right' average to use depends on the situation, and the nature of the data.

KEY POINTS

The results of the research

Tesco adapts through market research

'Our customers' lifestyles are changing. They work longer, value their free time more and have less time for shopping. Extended trading hours allow customers to shop when it is convenient for them.'

Source: Tesco plc annual review 1999

One way of classifying market research is to examine the information that it generates. This information may be:

- **controllable** – it is within the firm's power to alter a variable identified through research, such as poor packaging or an unsuitable method of promotion
- **uncontrollable** – the research identifies factors that are beyond the control of the firm, such as an economic downturn affecting sales and market size, or a new technological development influencing sales of its present model.

Progress check

1 Name **four** types of sampling method.
2 In what situations should a firm use (a) the mean, (b) the median and (c) the mode as the 'best' average?

2 (a) to determine what results from an equal distribution; (b) when order or ranking is important; (c) to identify the most commonly occurring values.

1 Random; quota; stratified; cluster.

5.3 New product development

After studying this section you should be able to:

- classify three types of 'new' product
- outline the stages in the development of new products
- explain how new product development can be supported

LEARNING SUMMARY

Stages in the development

AQA	M4
EDEXCEL	M4
OCR	M4
WJEC	M2
CCEA	M5

A product can be classed as 'new' if it is:

- **innovative** – it is the original model or type, such as the portable Sony Walkman, the Dyson vacuum cleaner which dispensed with the inner dust bag, and Nintendo's Game Boy
- **imitative** – products that copy the innovative original once it proves successful (the different makes of training shoe are a good example)
- **replacement** – where a new model of an existing product is brought out.

> It is estimated that less than 3% of all potential new products finally reach the market.

Innovative products result from efficient **research and development** (R&D) (page 125) and a **proactive** approach to product development: the firm seeks to be leader, attempting to create the market. This strategy carries the highest risk but also has the highest potential rewards, especially where the innovation can be protected, e.g. by a patent (page 127). The alternative approach, where imitative and replacement products are marketed, occurs where the firm is **reactive** and a market follower.

New product development has a number of stages.

1 Assess the demand	• *What does market research tell us?*
	• *Is the product feasible?*
	• *Is there a gap in the market?*
2 Obtain ideas	• *What can research and development suggest?*
	• *Who else can contribute ideas?*
3 Evaluate each idea	• *What does market research tell us?*
	• *Do the ideas fit the corporate plan?*
	• *What are the potential 'limiting factors'?*
	suppliers, demand, market size, break-even point,
	productive capacity, capital expenditure, etc.
4 Develop one idea	• *What resources do we need to develop the product?*
	• *What does the prototype look like?*
	• *What test marketing can we carry out?*
	• *What is the timetable for staff training, financial planning and equipment purchase?*
5 Launch the product	• *What forms of promotion do we need?*
	• *What does the test marketing tell us?*
	• *What is our pricing policy?*
6 Evaluate success	• *What is the consumer reaction?*

Supporting the development

AQA	M4
EDEXCEL	M4
OCR	M4
WJEC	M2
CCEA	M5

The first process of 'wide mesh' screening will eliminate many ideas on the grounds of funding or lack of expertise.

Two important areas of new product development are screening and test marketing. **Screening** takes place at the ideas evaluation stage. It analyses:

- labour availability and cost
- possible market reaction from competitors
- compatibility with –
  - corporate objectives
  - the existing product mix
- likely future market growth
- profit potential
- anticipated length of the life-cycle.

Test marketing relies on the production of prototypes or pilot products. The objective is to simulate as closely as possible the market, the product, and the marketing support that will be provided.

Even if the new product is successful, difficulties remain with its progress. These are:

- **high capital costs**
- **increased revenue expenditure** through having to retrain staff, hold additional stocks, a new advertising campaign, all of which affect the firm's liquidity position
- establishing and maintaining **new channels of distribution**
- difficulty in creating **consumer confidence** and loyalty.

Value analysis

The term **value engineering** is used when the focus is on manufacturing rather than on marketing.

To see whether their new (and existing) products are satisfying their consumers, e.g. in terms of style, design and functionality, firms may undertake **value analysis**. Value analysis involves staff in studying every feature of a product, to compare the **value** the feature adds against its **cost**. To do this properly usually requires an interdisciplinary approach, with expertise being required from production engineering, marketing and costing staff.

> Firms develop new products to maintain a balanced product mix.
>
> **KEY POINTS**

Progress check

1 Identify **three** types of 'new' product.

1 Innovative; imitative; replacement.

5.4 Sales forecasting

After studying this section you should be able to:

- distinguish between quantitative and qualitative sales forecasting techniques
- calculate trends and seasonal variations using time series analysis
- outline the major difficulties associated with sales forecasting

Nature and techniques

AQA	M4
EDEXCEL	M4, M5
OCR	M4
WJEC	M2
CCEA	M5

Sales forecasting seeks to estimate a firm's future sales, together with the related cash flows and profits. It can be short-term (tactical) for production planning, or for longer-term, strategic purposes such as estimating future staffing requirements.

Forecasters use **external** data by studying the industry as a whole and calculating the firm's estimated share of the total market, and **internal** sales statistics as a basis for the forecast.

Sales forecasting is complicated by the number of factors to be considered. Examples of these factors are:

External factors
- economic environment
- market research statistics
- market competition
- changing consumer tastes
- legislation

Internal factors
- previous sales statistics
- the firm's pricing policies
- its policies on offering discounts
- its distribution methods

Techniques for forecasting sales

Quantitative techniques include mathematical techniques such as **time series** analysis.

Qualitative techniques include:

- **test marketing** (page 70)
- **forecasting panels**, made up of sales force staff or other experts who give individual opinions on the likely sales, which can then be used to create a single forecast
- **user surveys** of existing customers and their expected future requirements.

Other quantitative techniques include **linear regression** analysis and **mathematical models**, created and manipulated using computers.

Difficulties with sales forecasting

The trend and seasonality patterns are not guaranteed to continue. Random variations that may be affecting trend and seasonal variations are ignored. The less data available on which the forecast is based, the less reliable the forecast will be.

STEP changes will also affect sales and other forecasting:

- **social** changes (tastes, fashion, environmental awareness etc.) make forecasting demand levels difficult
- **technological** changes in production methods affect costs and cost behaviour, making redundant the use of existing output and related statistics as a basis for forecasting
- **economic** and **political** changes, e.g. in interest rates, employment levels and policy, will affect forecasts made.

Key points from AS
- **Social influences**
  Revise AS pages 71–72
- **Technological influences**
  Revise AS page 72

> **KEY POINT**
>
> All forecasts are subject to error: the further the forecast into the future, the greater the error is likely to be.

Time series analysis

AQA	M4
EDEXCEL	M4, M5
OCR	M4
WJEC	M2
CCEA	M5

Examples may relate to seasons of the year (e.g. Xmas and toys), or may be shorter-term, e.g. weekly (for a shop, Saturday sales are normally higher than sales made on other days).

A 'time series' records figures over time. Typical examples for a firm involve analysing sales and factory output. Economic activity – recession, downturn, recovery and boom – can also be subjected to time series analysis.

The elements in time series analysis normally include:

- an identified **trend (T)** – an underlying long-term movement in the data over time
- **seasonal** variations **(S)** – shorter-term fluctuations due to seasonal or other factors
- **cyclical** variations **(C)** – fluctuations that take place in the longer term
- **random** variations **(I)** due to unforeseen, 'one-off', events.

> Time Series $Y = T + S (+ C + I)$ (normally the cyclical and random elements do not have to be calculated in questions).

KEY POINTS

The data are recorded on a **historigram**, with time on the horizontal axis and value on the vertical axis.

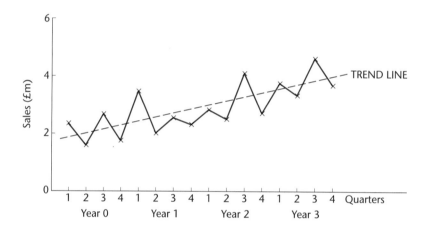

Finding the trend using moving averages

A **moving average** is the average of a set number of periods. It refers to the mid-point of the overall period. For example:

Month	Production (units)
0	3400
1	3200
2	4200
3	3700
4	3500
5	4500

Key points from AS

- **The business cycle**
  Revise AS page 60

A three-month moving average of monthly production is:

- **months 0–2** (3400 + 3200 + 4200) divided by 3 = 3600, which is located in the middle of the 3-month period (i.e. the middle of month 1)
- **months 1–3** (3200 + 4200 + 3700) divided by 3 = 3700 (the middle of month 2)
- **months 2–4** 11400 / 3 = 3800, located at the middle of month 3
- **months 3–5** 11700 / 3 = 3900.

This can be displayed:

Month	Production (units)	Moving total (3 months' sales)	Moving average
0	3400		
1	3200	10 800	3600
2	4200	11 100	3700
3	3700	11 400	3800
4	3500	11 700	3900
5	4500		

We can now clearly see the upward trend in monthly production, because the moving average column indicates the trend line.

Taking a moving average of an **even number** of time periods means the mid-point of the overall period won't refer to a single period. For example:

The **length** of the moving average period has to be selected: if there is a known cycle of seasonal variations (e.g. a year), the moving average should cover that cycle.

January	Sales	
week 1	48	
week 2	44	→ average 46
week 3	47	
week 4	45	

The average refers to the mid-point, between week 2 and week 3.

Finding the seasonal variation

Once the trend has been established, the seasonal variation can be calculated.

Since $Y = T + S + I$, then $Y - T = S + I$
(deducting the trend leaves the seasonal and random variations)

By making the assumption that the random variation is small and can therefore be ignored, the seasonal variation is:

$S = Y - T$

The seasonal variation is therefore the difference between the actual results and the trend. For example, the following data refers to a company's sales (in units):

	Quarter			
	1	*2*	*3*	*4*
Year 0	103	55	160	120
Year 1	107	59	167	130
Year 2	110	62	170	139

A weakness of calculating the moving average can be that it assumes the components remain independent, e.g. that an increasing trend doesn't increase the seasonal variation as well.

To calculate the moving average of the quarterly sales, a four-quarter moving total should be selected. Since the moving average first calculated won't be located against an actual quarter, a second moving average is taken, based on the mid-points of two moving averages as shown below. (The average has been rounded to the nearest whole number.) The seasonal variation is calculated as the difference between the actual sales and the trend.

Year	Quarter	Sales	Moving total (4 quarters)	Moving average (4 quarters)	Mid-point (of two moving averages) (TREND)	Seasonal variation
0	1	103				
	2	55				
			438	109.50		
	3	160			110	+50
			442	110.50		
	4	120			111	+9
			446	111.50		
1	1	107			112	-5
			453	113.25		
	2	59			114	-55
			463	115.75		
	3	167			116	+52
			466	116.50		
	4	130			117	+13
			469	117.25		
2	1	110			118	-8
			472	118.00		
	2	62			119	-57
			481	120.25		
	3	170				
	4	139				

The average seasonal variation is shown by re-displaying the calculations:

Year	Quarter 1	Quarter 2	Quarter 3	Quarter 4
0			+50	+9
1	−5	−55	+52	+13
2	−8	−57		
Total	−13	−112	+102	+22
Average	−6.5	−56	+51	+11

To deseasonalise – i.e. **seasonally adjust** – time series data, seasonal variations are removed to leave the trend.

Variations should cancel each other out, but −6.5 and −56 = −62.5, whereas +51 and +11 = +62. (The difference of −0.5 should be spread between the four unadjusted averages, to convert them to **adjusted averages**).

Using the information for forecasting

Time series analysis provides information to use in forecasting by:

- calculating moving averages to **find the trend**
- **extrapolating** the trend, i.e. projecting it forwards, outside the range of the data used
- **using the seasonal variation** to adjust the trend.

The trend line from the example can be plotted and extrapolated, and the seasonal variations added:

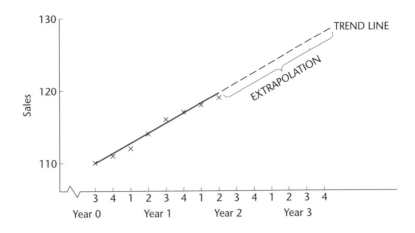

Forecast for year 3	Extrapolation	Seasonal adjustment	Forecast sales
Quarter 1	123	−6	117
Quarter 2	125	−56	68
Quarter 3	126	+51	176
Quarter 4	128	+11	139

Scattergraphs

A simple quantitative approach to forecasting is to use the scattergraph method:

- collect the data
- plot the data on a graph
- draw a line of best fit through the points.

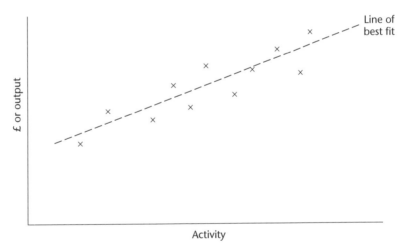

Figure 5.2 Example of a scattergraph

The main advantages of the scattergraph method are its **simplicity**, and its visual display of any **correlation** (relationship) between the items being plotted. Its major disadvantage is that it only gives an **approximation** of the exact position.

Progress check

1 In what ways is sales forecasting likely to prove limited and/or inaccurate?

2 How are time series seasonal variations calculated?

2 $S = Y − T$

1 Trend and seasonality patterns may not continue; random variations are ignored; the further the forecast into the future, the greater the likely error; the less data available, the less reliable the forecast will be; external (STEP) changes affect sales forecasting.

Sample question and model answer

1

JKL Ltd is considering employing a marketing specialist to help to identify new target markets. In order to grow, the firm needs to move away from a concentrated marketing strategy. Management realises that the firm has to consider where to position its products in the market. They feel that using market segmentation to develop a differentiated marketing strategy is the way forward for business.

(a) What is meant by:
   (i) 'target marketing' [2]
   (ii) 'positioning' [2]
   (iii) 'concentrated marketing' [2]
   (iv) 'market segmentation'? [2]

(b) Explain how the development of a brand name would be of benefit to JKL Ltd. [10]

(c) Evaluate the impact on JKL Ltd of using a differentiated marketing strategy. [12]

CCEA 1999, GCE A Level, Business Studies, Paper 1

(a) (i) The consumers at whom the firm is aiming its product or service.

   (ii) Positioning the product in the market, i.e. the firm analyses existing products in the market and places its product on the basis of at least two key characteristics such as price and image.

   (iii) This means the product is focused on only one or two particular market segments.

   (iv) The firm examines its overall market to study the different types of consumers buying its products, and then breaks it up (segments it) into different parts on this basis.

> Some very clear meanings given here: add an example of how segmentation takes place, e.g. by age or income.

(b) A brand name gives a clear focus for JKL to concentrate on when it is promoting its product. People associate the brand name with the image or unique product qualities JKL is promoting, e.g. its quality. This makes advertising more effective. Secondly, a successful brand name here will allow JKL to introduce new products under the same brand, which means that people buying the existing brand will have confidence about the new one, and be tempted to buy it. This is brand loyalty. Third, the brand name can be used defensively by JKL. If a new competitor enters the market, JKL's brand name can be used to maintain its market share. This is another illustration of how brand loyalty works.

> Again, the points are made very clearly. You could also point out that branding helps firms extend product life-cycles, and can make products more price inelastic (i.e. brand loyalty, where small price increases are tolerated, thereby increasing overall sales revenue).

(c) JKL is using a 'concentrated marketing strategy', in other words it is already using segmentation and concentrating on one market segment. By developing a differentiated marketing strategy, JKL will get involved in other market segments. To do this, however, there will be a cost consideration because a lot of market research into the new segments will be required. Linked to this is whether JKL is already producing a range of products that will appeal to different segments. If it isn't, it will again need to commit resources, e.g. to new product development. New products and new segments will require the company to consider its pricing strategy, to see what extent its current pricing strategy is suitable for the new segments (and new products if made). Finally, by moving into different markets or segments, JKL needs to examine its existing 'place' strategy, e.g. different channels of distribution may be required. What JKL must therefore do is to consider the overall 'marketing mix' when adopting a differentiated marketing strategy. There will be extra cost involved, e.g. through new product development and additional market research.

> A correct approach, analysing the influence of the marketing mix, but the answer ignores two crucial aspects. There is (a) the effect on other business functions (e.g. new staff needed, new production processes, new suppliers, the need to seek advice from government e.g. on exporting), and (b) the possible benefits of differentiation – e.g. reducing risk by diversifying into new products and new markets/different market segments.

Practice examination question

1 Read the following passage and then answer the questions that follow.

> **L'Oreal Paris**
>
> When Eugene Schueller invented the world's first synthetic hair dye back in 1907, he had second thoughts about names. He decided his new creation needed something more *à la mode*. One of the most fashionable hairstyles was L'Aureole. For M. Schueller that became L'Aureale and a few months later, L'Oreal which is not a million miles away from the Greek word 'orea' meaning beauty.

But what gives L'Oreal or more properly L'Oreal Paris its particular place in the portfolio of global brands? Perhaps it is because L'Oreal aims to present an image of elegance combined with a certain mystique. The company has spent heavily promoting the product being used by famous people, for example Jennifer Aniston and David Ginola. It seems to work because, according to L'Oreal , 36 per cent of British women said they had used at least one L'Oreal product in 1997. In 1999 the figure had risen to 48 per cent.

Once established, images can be oddly enduring. L'Oreal products reached Russia in 1914, three years before the revolution. Yet after the fall of communism, L'Oreal found its pre-revolutionary image virtually intact.

Cosmetics are big business to the extent of some 3 billion units, for example in lipsticks, mascara, nail enamels, foundation and blusher of which the United States accounts for a third.

(a) Explain **two** factors that a company like L'Oreal Paris needs to consider when choosing a famous person to promote one of its brands. [4]

(b) How can a business such as L'Oreal Paris be successful despite charging premium prices in a competitive market? [6]

(c) Assess the key factors, which a global business such as L'Oreal Paris, will need to take into account in developing its marketing strategy. [8]

WJEC Module 2 paper 2000

Chapter 6

Accounting and finance

The following topics are covered in this chapter:

- *Financial information*
- *Key features of final accounts*
- *Interpreting final accounts*

- *Investment decision-making*
- *Cost analysis and decision-making*
- *Contribution and marginal costing*

6.1 Financial information

After studying this section you should be able to:

- *identify the issues affecting choice of the source of finance*
- *state the main elements of financial accounting*
- *describe, and give a relevant business example of, the main accounting concepts*

Sources of finance

AQA	AS
EDEXCEL	AS
OCR	M5
WJEC	AS
CCEA	AS

Key points from AS

- **Sources of finance**
  Revise AS page 82–83

The key questions that managers have to answer are:

- **how much** finance is needed
- whether it can be obtained **internally**
- whether it should be borrowed **temporarily**, with a view to paying back, or obtained as **permanent** (e.g. share) capital
- (if borrowed) whether the loan is for the **short** (up to one year), **medium** (1–5 years) or **long** term.

The amount and nature of this finance varies from firm to firm, and is influenced by a firm's **size**, its form of **ownership**, the type of **technology** currently being used within the firm, the relationship between **capital and labour**, the length of **credit periods** (taken and allowed), and the age of the firm's **assets**.

Elements and users of financial information

AQA	M4
EDEXCEL	M4
OCR	M5
WJEC	M3
CCEA	M4

Financial accounting deals with **external influences** on the firm, whereas management accounting provides an **internal analysis** of the firm's operations.

Stakeholders use financial information. They may be:

- **internal** (management and employees) or
- **external**, e.g. suppliers, customers, lenders.

In December 1999 the **Accounting Standards Board (ASB)** published its *Statement of Principles for Financial Reporting*. Although not a financial accounting standard as such, this influential Statement provides guidance in applying financial accounting standards, and identifies the key **elements** of financial statements as:

- **Assets** and **Liabilities**
- **Ownership interest** (the 'accounting equation' of Assets minus Liabilities)
- **Gains** and **Losses** (income and expenses)
- **Contributions from owners** (investments) and **Distributions to owners**.

Key points from AS

- **The nature and purpose of accounting**
  Revise AS page 75
- **Types of accounts**
  Revise AS page 76

Accounting concepts

Accounting concepts act as basic 'rules' for accountants to follow. One of the financial accounting 'standards', *SSAP 2 (Disclosure of Accounting Policies)*, identifies four key concepts.

- **Accruals** – financial accounts are prepared not on a cash basis but on an **earnings** (accruals) basis. Sales and purchases are recognised in the period in which they are made, and not merely when the cash is received or paid. Therefore, a company with a financial year running January–December and making a credit sale in December 2001, but not receiving the cash until January 2002, will show the sale as increasing its 2001 profits.
- **Prudence** – where alternative procedures or valuations are possible, the one selected should give the **most cautious** presentation of the firm's financial state. Losses therefore tend to be anticipated, but profits are never anticipated (this is why, for example, closing stock is valued at cost price rather than selling price: to value using the latter figure assumes the stock will be sold and a profit made).
- **Going concern** – the assumption is that the firm will continue for the foreseeable future. This means that its assets will normally be valued at their (historical) cost rather than at their break-up or resale value.
- **Consistency** – similar items should be given similar accounting treatment. If, therefore, it is the firm's policy to use the straight-line depreciation method for existing vehicles, any new vehicle bought will be subject to the same treatment.

Other relevant accounting concepts

- The **entity** concept – accountants treat every business as an entity which is separate to, and distinct from, its owners.
- The **money measurement** concept – accounts only record and analyse those items that have a monetary value (thus, for example, the quality of management and other employees is not directly considered by accountants).
- The **duality** concept – every transaction has two effects (this forms the basis of **double-entry book-keeping**).
- The **historical cost** concept – items are normally stated in accounts at their historical cost, i.e. the cost that was paid for them (revaluation can take place, e.g. property is often shown at a higher value than its original cost).
- The **materiality** concept – only items that are sufficiently material (important) will affect the 'true and fair view' that must be given by accounts.

These concepts provide a degree of **objectivity** in financial accounting: using historical cost for all items is a good example of this. The materiality concept illustrates where financial accounts may still be **subjective**: what is 'material' in one firm may not be regarded as material by the accountant in another firm.

The accountant's view here differs from the legal one with regard to sole traders and partnerships (see page 32).

A good example is where small, long-lasting items such as waste-paper bins (technically fixed assets) are treated as revenue, rather than capital, expenditure.

> Financial accounting applies rules in an attempt to make it more objective, though a degree of subjectivity still exists.
>
> **KEY POINTS**

6.2 Key features of final accounts

After studying this section you should be able to:

- *distinguish between the profit and loss account and the balance sheet*
- *explain the purpose, and effect, of depreciation in final accounts*
- *outline the reasons for distinguishing between capital and revenue expenditure*

LEARNING SUMMARY

The financial statements

AQA	M4
EDEXCEL	M4
OCR	M5
WJEC	M3
CCEA	M4

Key points from AS

- **Final accounts**
  Revise AS pages 76–78
- **Capital and revenue expenditure**
  Revise AS page 78
- **Depreciation in final accounts**
  Revise AS page 79

UK law recognises a company as a separate legal 'person', an entity that is distinct from its owners. It can therefore sue and be sued, and take out contracts in its own name. Sole traders and partnerships, however, are not separate entities from their owners in the eyes of the law. In financial accounting, the (**business**) **entity** concept requires accountants to treat **all** businesses – including sole traders and partnerships – as separate entities from their owners.

The main financial statements are the **profit and loss account** and the **balance sheet**.

Profit and loss account
- is an **income** statement
- shows calculation of **profit**
- information from **expense** and **revenue** accounts

Balance sheet
- shows **net assets** and **capital employed**
- summarises the **financial position**
- information from **asset** and **liability** accounts

Depreciation in financial statements

Depreciation is a non-cash expense, which is taken into consideration when the firm's cash flow (its third major financial statement) is calculated.

The **consistency** concept ensures that the same calculation method – straight line, reducing balance and revaluation are the most popular ones – will normally be used for similar assets. The **accruals** concept, where costs are **matched** to the period to which they refer, means that each year's profit will be charged with its own share of the total depreciation. The firm can change its depreciation policy and method of calculation, but only for good reason.

The purpose of applying depreciation is therefore to adjust annual profits, to avoid charging the full amount of depreciation in a single year (which would distort that year's profits). This leads to a **fairer comparison** between the profit figures for the years over which the asset is owned.

Depreciation is **subjective**: the accountant has to decide which method of calculation to use. If selecting the straight-line method, decisions must be made concerning two of the three figures involved in the calculation (the estimated life of the asset, and its expected resale value); if the reducing balance method is used, the percentage written down each year must be decided.

A provision is defined as 'a liability of uncertain amount': the exact figure at the time is not known with certainty.

Since depreciation is a **provision**, an adjustment will be made when the asset is disposed of. The firm will make either a loss or a profit on sale, which is recorded in the profit and loss account. Over the full life of the asset, the total depreciation charged will be the same **regardless** of method selected and amounts charged, because of this final adjustment. For this reason, total profits over the asset's life will also be the same, even though the individual figures will vary.

Capital and revenue expenditure in financial statements

Capital expenditure	*Revenue expenditure*
appears in the balance sheet	appears in the profit and loss account

The key concepts influencing a firm's approach to classifying expenditure are accruals, consistency and materiality.

This is an important distinction in the financial statements because:

If revenue expenditure is wrongly classified as capital expenditure:

- expenses will be understated
- net profit will be overstated

If capital expenditure is wrongly classified as revenue expenditure:

- expenses will be overstated
- net profit will be understated

Capital expenditure does not affect profit calculation: revenue expenditure does.

KEY POINTS

Progress check

1 Give an example of how fixed asset valuations and their depreciation are influenced by each of these concepts:

(a) consistency

(b) prudence

(c) going concern.

1 (a) New assets are recorded at historic cost (consistent), and the same method of depreciation is used for each class of asset; (b) the most cautious method of depreciation is used (which will not overstate the asset value); (c) fixed assets stay recorded at their historic cost, not their resale or break-up value.

6.3 Interpreting final accounts

After studying this section you should be able to:

- *explain the difference between profitability, liquidity, efficiency and debt/gearing*
- *calculate the main accounting ratios*
- *reach appropriate conclusions on the basis of your calculations*

LEARNING SUMMARY

Final accounts and their interpretation

AQA	M4
EDEXCEL	M4
OCR	M5
WJEC	M3
CCEA	M4

Accounting ratios are important indicators in **benchmarking** (page 44).

Although accounts must be kept for external purposes, e.g. to assess and calculate the firm's tax bill, one result of keeping these financial records is to allow analysis to take place. This analysis has:

- an **internal focus**, when the firm compares its present performance with past records in order to establish **trends** and to indicate **efficiency**
- an **external** focus, when the firm assesses its **competitiveness** by comparing results with other organisations in the same industry.

Profitability

Profitability measures a firm's **total profit against the resources used** in making that profit. On its own, profit is a relatively meaningless figure: it needs comparing against figures such as **turnover** and **capital employed**.

Profitability ratios

1 Return on capital employed (ROCE) $\dfrac{net\ profit}{capital\ employed} \times 100$

This shows the profitability of the investment by calculating its percentage return. The return shown can then be compared with the expected return from other investments. The normal figure used by companies is profit on ordinary activities before taxation rather than after tax (the tax charge may vary from year to year, so using profit after tax would not lead to comparing like with like). If **PBIT** – profit before interest and tax – is used, the profit figure is compared with **capital employed**, i.e. share capital plus long-term loan capital.

ROCE can be sub-divided:

Capital employed = net assets, so the figure of capital employed used in the calculation equates to net assets (assets less liabilities).

ROCE	=	Profit margin	×	Asset turnover
$\dfrac{PBIT}{capital\ employed}$	=	$\dfrac{PBIT}{sales}$	×	$\dfrac{sales}{capital\ employed}$

The **profit margin** ratio (see below) shows whether the company is making a low or a high profit margin on its sales; the **asset turnover** ratio measures how efficiently the company's net assets are being used to generate its sales.

2 Gross profit margin (GP ratio, or GP %) $\dfrac{gross\ profit}{turnover} \times 100$

This indicates the percentage of **turnover** – net sales (sales less VAT and any returns) – represented by gross profit. If the gross profit margin is 30%, this means the firm's **cost of sales** are 70% of its turnover (because turnover = cost of sales + gross profit).

Key points from AS

- **Accounting ratios**
  Revise AS pages 80–81

3 Net profit margin (NP ratio, or NP %) $\dfrac{net\ profit}{turnover} \times 100$

This shows the percentage of turnover represented by net profit, i.e. how many pence out of every £1 sold is net profit. The NP margin will fall if the GP margin has fallen and rise if the GP% has increased: but it is also affected when the firm's other expenses as a percentage of turnover have changed.

Liquidity

Liquidity is **the amount of cash a firm can get quickly in order to settle its immediate debts**. Although a firm can survive in the short term without profit, it cannot survive for long without sufficient liquidity. Liquid funds consist of:

- cash in hand and at bank
- short-term investments and deposits
- trade debtors.

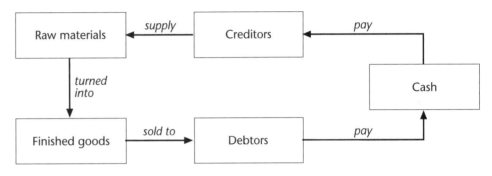

Fig 6.1 The cash (or 'operating') cycle

An efficient **credit control** system is particularly important in ensuring cash flows into the firm remain constant and efficient.

Examining the cash cycle shows the following:

- the timing of cash flows will not necessarily coincide with sales and purchases (cost of sales) – allowing and taking credit will cause this difference
- delays also occur with cash receipts, through allowing credit or increasing the credit period, and by holding additional stock
- cash payments may be delayed through taking credit.

Liquidity ratios

Liquidity ratios help establish whether a firm is **overtrading**, expanding without sufficient long-term capital. This puts pressure on its **working capital**, the **excess of current assets over current liabilities**.

A firm may also have too high a level of working capital, indicating that liquid assets are not being used productively (e.g. they are tied up in surplus stocks).

1 Working capital (current) ratio   *current assets (CA):current liabilities (CL)*

If current liabilities exceed current assets, the firm may have difficulty in meeting its debts. Extra short-term borrowing, to pay off creditors, costs the firm money (interest). If the firm sells assets to help meet its debts, it risks loss of production and future expansion.

2 Liquid ratio ('Acid test' or 'Quick assets')   *CA minus stock:CL*

Using this ratio lets us see whether the firm can meet short-term debts without having to sell stock, which is regarded as the least liquid current asset (and the prudence concept encourages accountants to assume the firm will not automatically sell – **realise** – its stock).

3 Debtors' collection period ('Debtor days') $\dfrac{debtors}{sales} \times 365$

This liquidity (or efficiency) ratio shows the time, measured in average days, that it takes debtors to pay the firm.

We have to be careful to ensure the debtors and creditors figures we use are representative (i.e. typical) totals.

4 Creditors' collection period ('Creditor days') $\dfrac{creditors}{purchases} \times 365$

This ratio calculates the average length of credit the firm receives from its suppliers.

'Window dressing'

This term is used to describe techniques for **improving a company's balance sheet position**, in particular its apparent liquidity. Examples include:

- paying additional money into the bank account just before the year end, in order to boost the cash balance (the amount is then withdrawn later)
- using inter-group transfers – one cash-rich company in a group forwards a cheque to another group company with an overdraft, then cancels the cheque after the year end (this hides the other company's overdraft, which would otherwise have to be shown in the group accounts)
- undertaking sale and leaseback just before the year end.

SSAP 17, Accounting for post balance sheet events, helps control window dressing by forcing companies to reverse transactions taken before the year end, if these transactions were made to alter the appearance of the company's balance sheet.

> **Liquidity,** associated with cash flow, measures the firm's ability to survive in the short run. **Profitability** is a clearer indicator of its ability to survive in the longer term.
>
> **KEY POINTS**

Asset efficiency

Firms need to use their assets as efficiently as possible. The efficiency of both current and fixed assets can be measured.

Asset efficiency ratios

1 **Rate of stock turnover ('Stockturn')** $\quad \dfrac{cost\ of\ sales}{average\ stock} \quad$ *(stated as ' ... times per period')*

Stock must be valued at the **lower of cost or net realisable value** (another example of the Prudence concept in operation).

The purpose is to calculate how frequently the firm sells its stock: if stock turnover is slowing, the firm is holding more stock than before, it may be facing problems selling its products, or it may have bought additional stock to take advantage of discounts offered.

An alternative calculation to display 'stock days' is $\quad \dfrac{average\ stock}{cost\ of\ sales} \times 365$

This is a useful analysis when used in conjunction with debtor days and creditor days in showing cash-flow timings.

2 **Asset turnover** $\quad \dfrac{sales}{net\ assets}$

This 'secondary ratio' from ROCE (see above) assesses the value of sales generated by the net assets representing the capital being employed in the firm. It illustrates how efficiently the firm is using its assets to generate turnover.

Debt and gearing

The debt ratios show **how much the company owes in relation to its size**. This analysis indicates whether lenders are likely to loan additional funds given the level of the company's debt. **Gearing** is important when additional capital is required. If a company is already highly geared, it may find it difficult to take out further loans. Also, the more highly geared the company, the greater the risk that the shareholders will not receive a dividend distribution. A highly geared company having external loans may find that, because it must pay a large amount of interest annually, the lenders force it to sell assets to generate payments: if their loans are secured on assets, they may remove the assets if interest payments are not met.

Debt and gearing ratios

1 Debt ratio   *Ratio of total debts to total assets*

50% is often regarded as the generally accepted maximum figure: again, an important consideration is whether this figure is rising or falling.

2 Gearing $\dfrac{prior\ charge\ capital}{total\ long\text{-}term\ capital}$ *(long-term loans + preference shares)*

This analyses the different types of payments made to capital. Companies with more than 50% prior charge capital are called 'high-geared': those with less than 50% are 'low-geared'.

3 Debt/equity ratio $\dfrac{prior\ charge\ capital}{ordinary\ share\ capital + reserves}$

This gives similar information to the gearing ratio.

4 Interest cover $\dfrac{PBIT}{interest\ charges}$

The interest cover ratio shows if the company is making sufficient profits (before interest and tax) in order to pay interest costs easily.

> An interest cover of at least 3 is normally expected, and a figure below 2 is regarded as low.

> **KEY POINTS**
>
> A company's gearing should be assessed from the differing viewpoints of the directors, the investors (shareholders), and the actual and potential lenders.

Investment

Actual and potential shareholders are interested in assessing the value of an investment in (ordinary) shares of a company. Since the value of a **listed company** is its market value, some of these ratios take account of the share price as well as the information in the published accounts.

Shareholders are normally interested in two aspects of their investment:

- the **share price** (any increase here provides **capital** growth), and
- the **dividend received**, which forms the **income** element.

As a result, companies can often be under pressure to adopt policies that will ensure **adequate short-term profits** (e.g. to finance dividend distribution): this may conflict with their **plans for long-term growth**.

Investment ratios

1 Earnings per share (EPS) $\dfrac{profit\ available\ for\ ordinary\ shareholders}{number\ of\ ordinary\ shares}$

This represents the return on each ordinary share, and is nowadays stated in the published accounts.

2 Dividend cover $\dfrac{EPS}{net\ dividend\ per\ ordinary\ share}$

> Dividend per share will be stated in pence per share.

The dividend cover shows that proportion of profit available for ordinary shareholders which has been distributed, and that proportion which has been retained to help fund future growth. For example, a cover of two times indicates half the available profits have been distributed and half retained.

3 Price/earnings (P/E) ratio   *Ratio of the current share price to the EPS*

The higher the P/E ratio, the greater the confidence shareholders have in the company. It is particularly important to compare this ratio to those of other companies in the same industry.

In practice, the previous year's share dividend can be used to calculate this ratio.

4 Dividend yield $\dfrac{\textit{share dividend for the year}}{\textit{current market value of the share (ex dividend)}}$

This indicates the return the shareholder is expecting on the share.

Examples of final accounts

AQA	M4
EDEXCEL	M4
OCR	M5
WJEC	M3
CCEA	M4

The ASB's Statement (page 78) outlines the **components** of financial statements. These are the:

- profit and loss account
- balance sheet
- cash flow statement
- statement of total recognised gains and losses.

Here is an example of each of these statements.

Consolidated Profit and Loss Account
for the 52 weeks ended 29 January 2000

	2000 £'000	1999 £'000
Turnover		
Continuing operations	203,769	205,710
Discontinued operations	15,913	30,364
	219,682	236,074
Operating profit		
Continuing operations	16,263	14,143
Discontinued operations	1,439	2,487
	17,702	16,630
Net profit on disposals of discontinued operations		
Profit on disposal of discontinued operations, before goodwill write back	26,984	–
Goodwill written back	(6,721)	–
Profit on disposal after goodwill write back	20,263	–
Profit on sale of properties	1,209	–
Profit before investment income and interest	39,174	16,630
Share of operating profit of associate	20	14
Profit on ordinary activities before interest	39,194	16,644
Net interest receivable/(payable)	819	(355)
Profit on ordinary activities before taxation	40,013	16,289
Tax on profit on ordinary activities	(14,531)	(5,278)
Profit for the financial year	25,482	11,011
Dividends	(5,839)	(5,431)
Retained profit for the financial year	19,643	5,580
Earnings per share	28.90p	24.33p

Figure 6.2 *Summarised profit and loss account*   Source: Silentnight Holdings plc, 2000

'Consolidated' refers to combining the final accounts of different companies in the group. Reading the account shows us that:

- discontinued (finishing) operations are analysed separately
- profits can be made (e.g. on sale of properties) other than through trading
- there are a number of different profit figures calculated – **operating profit** is a particularly important figure
- retained profit is shown as the final amount
- EPS is stated at the end of this account.

Consolidated Balance Sheet
at 29 January 2000

	2000 £'000	1999 £'000
Fixed assets		
Intangible assets		
Tangible assets	–	1,932
Investments	43,057	54,240
	4,076	4,028
	47,133	60,200
Current assets		
Stocks	10,974	13,913
Debtors	28,945	33,177
Cash at bank and in hand	46,334	12,666
	86,253	59,756
Creditors: amounts falling due within one year	43,223	44,832
Net current assets	43,030	14,924
Total assets less current liabilities	90,163	75,124
Creditors: amounts falling due after more than one year	2,789	13,562
Provision for liabilities and charges	180	185
	2,969	13,747
Net assets	87,194	61,377
Capital and reserves		
Called up share capital	4,685	4,685
Share premium account	1,084	1,084
Revaluation reserve	4,767	4,911
Profit and loss account	76,658	50,697
Equity shareholders' funds	87,194	61,377

Figure 6.3 *Summarised balance sheet*   Source: Silentnight Holdings plc, 2000

Studying this statement shows us that:

- assets and liabilities are classified and the main categories shown
- net current assets (working capital) is clearly displayed
- the net assets total equals that of equity shareholders' funds (capital employed), i.e. capital equals assets less liabilities.

Consolidated Cash Flow Statement
for the 52 weeks ended 29 January 2000

	2000 £'000	2000 £'000	1999 £'000	1999 £'000
Net cash inflow from operating activities		24,477		24,521
Dividends received from associate		34		55
Returns on investments and servicing of finance				
Interest received	1,059		273	
Interest paid	(213)		(611)	
Interest element of finance leases	(27)		(57)	
		819		(395)
Taxation		(12,194)		(5,919)
Capital expenditure and financial investment				
Purchase of fixed assets	(7,444)		(14,095)	
Sale of fixed assets	535		523	
Proceeds from sale of properties	4,012		–	
Sale of shares by Executive Share Option Scheme	497		346	
Purchase of own shares on behalf of Executive Share Option Scheme	(558)		(425)	
		(2,958)		(13,651)
Acquisitions and disposals				
Deferred consideration on acquisition in prior year	–		(652)	
Proceeds of sale of discontinued operations net of cash balances at disposals	34,112		–	
		34,112		(652)
Equity dividends paid		(5,521)		(5,386)
Net cash inflow/(outflow) before management of liquid resources and financing		38,769		(1,427)
Management of liquid resources				
Increase in short term cash deposits		(28,259)		(2,474)
Financing				
Issue of ordinary shares	–		1	
Repayment of bank loans	(4,900)		(73)	
New bank loans	–		5,488	
Capital element of finance lease rental payments	(197)		(262)	
		(5,097)		5,154
Increase in cash		5,413		1,253

Figure 6.4 Cash flow statement Source: Silentnight Holdings plc, 2000

This statement details the cash movements that have taken place during the year. The less self-explanatory sections are:

- net cash inflow from operating activities – essentially, cash generated through trading
- acquisitions and disposals (of other businesses)
- equity dividends paid (to ordinary shareholders)
- financing (major capital movements).

The overall increase in cash forms part of the 'Cash at bank and in hand' figure for the balance sheet.

Consolidated Statement of Total Recognised Gains and Losses
for the 52 weeks ended 29 January 2000

	2000 £'000	1999 £'000
Profit for the financial year	25,482	11,011
Currency translation differences on foreign currency net investments	(547)	146
Total recognised gains and losses for the financial year	24,935	11,157

Figure 6.5 Statement of total recognised gains and losses   Source: Silentnight Holdings plc, 2000

This statement is provided in order to analyse the non-trading profits and losses that occur in large companies.

The five year summary

This is another feature of modern financial statements. Sometimes the summary just lists the main profit and loss and balance categories: other summaries, such as this illustration, provide financial ratio analysis.

Financial statistics years ended 31 March

Financial ratios	1996	1997	1998	1999	2000
Basic earnings per share – pence	31.6	32.8	26.6	46.3	31.7
Growth in dividends per share % (a)	5.6	6.1	6.4	7.4	7.4
Return on capital employed % (b)	18.4	19.1	19.5	19.2	18.2
Gearing – net debt to equity % (c)	7.4	1.6	36.1	6.3	53.4
Interest cover (d)	16.9	19.7	11.2	12.2	8.8
Dividend cover (a) (e)	1.7	1.7	1.8	1.7	1.4

(a) 1997 and 1998 figures exclude the effects of the special dividend of 35p per share paid in September 1997.

(b) The ratio is based on profit before tax, goodwill, amortisation and interest on long-term borrowings, to average capital employed. Capital employed is represented by total assets, excluding goodwill, less current liabilities, excluding corporate taxes and dividends payable, and provisions other than those for deferred taxation. Year-end figures are used in the computation of the average, except in the case of short-term investments and borrowings where average daily balances are used in their place.

(c) The ratio is based on borrowings net of cash and short-term investments to capital and reserves and minority interests.

(d) The number of times net interest payable is covered by operating profit before goodwill amortisation. In 1997, net interest excludes the premium paid on the repurchase of bonds.

(e) The number of times dividends are covered by earnings. The figure for 1998 excludes the effect of the windfall tax charge and the figure for 1999 excludes the gain on sale of the MCI shares.

Figure 6.6 Five year summary   Source: British telecommunications plc, 2000

Limitations of final accounts

Although ratios can show key trends, ratio analysis on its own is not a sufficiently detailed guide to a firm's performance. For companies, additional information comes from:

- analysing the chairman's and directors' reports
- reviewing the age and type of assets
- assessing the company's markets.

Even this analysis will not provide the full picture, however. One key reason for this is that financial accounting information is **historic** in nature, looking back rather than forwards. As a result, accurate projections may not be made easily from the analysis. Also, financial accounting (through applying the money measurement concept) concentrates only on those items to which a monetary value can be made. This is again an incomplete analysis, ignoring factors such as the likely obsolescence of the company's main product, and the strength of its market share and competition.

> Financial statements are analysed using ratios, the results of which can be used for inter-firm comparisons and to identify trends.

KEY POINTS

Progress check

1 Merchant Ltd buys raw materials on five weeks' credit, issues them after a week's storage and takes another three weeks to turn them into finished products. These products are stored for another week, then sold to debtors who pay in a further four weeks. What is the length of the cash cycle?

2 During a year, a business bought stock costing £40 000: stock at the start of the year was £5000 and at the end of the year £11 000. What was the stock-turn?

3 Outline the nature and purpose of the three main financial statements.

3 Profit and loss account: contains revenues and expenses, shows profit. Balance sheet: summarises the firm's financial position. Cash flow statement: analyses cash movements.

2 5 times (£40 000/£8000 average stock).

1 week storage + 3 weeks production + 1 week storage + 4 weeks to pay = 9 weeks; deduct 5 weeks credit from suppliers = 4 weeks.

6.4 Investment decision-making

After studying this section you should be able to:

- *explain the difference between the payback, average rate of return, and discounted cash flow methods of investment appraisal*
- *apply each method to given data and reach appropriate conclusions*

LEARNING SUMMARY

Capital investment decisions

AQA	M4
EDEXCEL	M4
OCR	M5
WJEC	M3
CCEA	M4

These calculations also help decisions to be made between alternative capital projects.

Because of the major capital outlay involved, managers try to calculate **expected profitability** and **expected cash flows** for the proposed investment. They use three methods of investment appraisal.

Payback period method

This method of investment appraisal calculates how long it takes a project to repay its original investment. The method therefore concentrates on **cash flow**, highlighting projects that recover quickly their initial investment. Here is an example of how it works.

A company is considering two different capital investment projects. Both are expected to operate for four years. Only one of the projects can be financed.

	Project A (£)	Project B (£)
Initial cost	**22 000**	**22 000**
Profit/(loss):		
year 1	2000	2500
year 2	4000	1500
year 3	7000	3000
year 4	(3000)	5000
Expected scrap value	2000	2000
Annual depreciation	5000	5000

The payback periods are calculated by adding annual depreciation back to the cash flows: depreciation is a **non-cash expense** that reduces profit, and so the profit figures given understate the cash inflows by the amount of the depreciation. Cash flow in year 4 is also increased by the scrap values for each project.

Year	Project A		Project B	
	Annual cash flow (£)	Cumulative cash flow (£)	Annual cash flow (£)	Cumulative cash flow (£)
0	(22 000)	(22 000)	(22 000)	(22 000)
1	7 000	(15 000)	7 500	(14 500)
2	9 000	(6 000)	6 500	(8 000)
3	12 000	6 000	8 000	—
4	4 000	10 000	12 000	12 000

Although the payback method is widely used in practice, it is often as a supplement to the other, more sophisticated, appraisal methods.

The payback period for project A is two and a half years. At the start of year 3, outflows exceed inflows by £6000. Net inflows for year 3 are £12 000 (£1000 per month): it therefore recoups its original investment after six months of year 3. Project B's payback period is three years. The manager would therefore select project A on the basis of this method, even though project B generates a greater total cash inflow by the end of its life.

- This method is easy to calculate and understand.
- Its use emphasises **liquidity**, because calculations are based solely on cash flow.
- It also helps managers to **reduce risk** by selecting the project that recovers its outlay most quickly.
- Early cash flows can be predicted more accurately than later ones, and are less affected by inflation.

The main drawback of this method is that it completely **ignores profit and profitability**. It also takes no account of interest rates.

Accounting rate of return (ARR) method

This method is also known by the name 'return on investment'.

This method of investment appraisal calculates the **expected profits** from the investment, expressing them as a percentage of the capital invested. The higher the rate of return, the 'better' (i.e. the more profitable) is the project. The ARR is therefore based on anticipated profits rather than on cash flow.

$$ARR = \frac{\text{expected average profits}}{\text{original investment}} \times 100$$

Using the above figures, project A generates total profits of £10 000 and project B total profits of £12 000.

Project A (£)	Project B (£)
2500	3000
22 000	22 000
ARR = 11.4%	ARR = 13.6%

Project B would therefore be selected using ARR.

- The accounting rate of return method is easy to use and simple to understand.
- It measures and highlights the **profitability** of each project.

Its disadvantages are that **it ignores the timing of a project's contributions**. High profits in the early years – which can be estimated more accurately, and which help minimise the project's risk – are treated in the same way as profits occurring later. It also concentrates on profits rather than cash flows, **ignoring the time value of money** (profits in the later years being eroded by the effects of inflation).

Discounted cash flow (DCF) method

DCF assumes that a firm prefers to use cash in year 1 rather than in year 2, because **the earlier the cash is received, the sooner it can be reinvested.**

The principle of DCF is based on using discounted arithmetic to get a **present value for future cash inflows and outflows**. This method is sometimes divided into two elements, which complement each other:

- the **net present value (NPV)** method, which takes account of all relevant cash flows from the project throughout its life, discounting them to their 'present value'
- the **internal rate of return (IRR)** method, which compares the rate of return expected from the project with that identified by the company as being the cost of its capital – projects having an IRR that exceeds the cost of capital are worth considering.

As an example, a company receiving £100 at the start of a year might be able to invest it at 10% *per annum*: by the end of the year this investment will be worth £110. Given the choice of £100 now or a higher sum in a year's time, the managers will choose the higher sum only if it exceeds £110. This principle works in reverse: the managers know that a project generating £110 in a year's time is worth the same as one generating £100 immediately, the project with the future value being discounted to its present value (by using a set of discounting tables).

The NPV method calculates the **present value of the project's future cash flows**. Each year's cash flow is discounted to a present value, which shows how much the managers would have to invest now at a given rate of interest to earn these future cash benefits. The present value of the total cash outflows is compared to that of the total cash inflows to calculate the **net present value** of the project. The project with the highest positive NPV will be chosen.

- **If the NPV is positive** – cash benefits exceed cash costs – this means that the project will earn a return in excess of its cost of capital (the rate of interest/discounting used in the calculations).
- **If the NPV is negative**, this means the cost of investing in the project exceeds the present value of future receipts, and so it is not worth investing in it.

If the company planning to invest in either project A or B has a cost of capital equal to 12%, the future cash flows can be discounted to their present values using discounting tables. The present value of £1 when discounted at 12% is:

Thus £1 in a year's time is the same as 89.3p invested now at 12% for one year; £1 in two years' time is the same as 79.7p invested at 12% over 2 years, etc.

Year	Present value (PV) factor 12%
0	1.000
1	0.893
2	0.797
3	0.712
4	0.636

Year	Project A			Project B		
	Cash flow	PV factor	NPV	Cash flow	PV factor	NPV
0	(22 000)	1.000	(22000)	(22000)	1.000	(22000)
1	7000	0.893	6251	7500	0.893	6698
2	9000	0.797	7173	6500	0.797	5180
3	12000	0.712	8544	8000	0.712	5696
4	4000	0.636	2544	12000	0.636	7632
		NPV =	2512		NPV =	3206

Project B has the higher expected NPV and would therefore be selected.

The IRR method involves comparing the actual rates of return – in this illustration, both rates exceed 12% since both show positive NPVs when discounted at 12% – with the company's cost of capital.

If the cost of capital is 12%, both projects are worth undertaking if possible, because the average annual returns on capital are above the 12% figure.

The use of DCF takes account of all cash flows, and it acknowledges the time value of money. The main problem is in **establishing a suitable discount rate** to use, because this rate (and the firm's cost of capital) is likely to vary over the life of the project.

KEY POINTS

Organisations undertake investment appraisal to evaluate the likely success and value of capital investments, which tie up the firm's finance for a long period, normally for a number of years.

Progress check

1 Which appraisal method concentrates on (a) liquidity (b) profitability?

2 Why are profit figures adjusted for depreciation when calculating payback?

2 Depreciation is a non-cash expense that has reduced profit: to get the cash-flow equivalent, depreciation must be added back to the profit figure.

1 (a) payback; (b) ARR.

6.5 Cost analysis and decision-making

After studying this section you should be able to:

- classify and analyse a range of costs
- evaluate absorption costing, budgetary control and standard costing as control and planning methods

LEARNING SUMMARY

Absorption costing

AQA A	AS
EDEXCEL	M4
OCR	M5
WJEC	M3
CCEA	M4

Companies not in traditional manufacturing may use **activity-based costing** (ABC): it uses 'cost drivers' based on its major non-manufacturing activities (e.g. ordering, despatch) to absorb overheads.

Allocation, apportionment and absorption

Overheads are **allocated** when the cost is incurred wholly by a **single department** or **cost centre**. The overhead can then be charged exclusively to that cost centre. Overheads have to be **apportioned** when the cost is incurred by **more than one** cost centre. A good example is factory rent, with the total cost having to be shared between all relevant cost centres in the factory.

The **basis of apportionment** will vary according to the nature of the overhead. For example:

Overhead	Possible basis of apportionment
Rent and rates	Floor area
Lighting and heating	Volume or floor area
Equipment depreciation	Cost or book value of equipment
Maintenance staff	Hours clocked for each department
Stores staff	Value of material requisitions
Administrative support:	
e.g. personnel and canteen costs	Number of employees

In absorption costing, all overheads (indirect costs) must be **absorbed**, i.e. **recovered**, by the products, otherwise there will be no source of income to pay for these overheads. For example, if a product's share of total overheads comes to £300 000, this amount needs to be recovered throughout the period when the product is sold.

Absorption methods include:

- **direct labour hours** – e.g. in a garage, if the budgeted number of direct labour hours is 100 000, each hour spent working on a car will be charged with an extra £3 (i.e. £300 000/100 000), so by the end of the period the £300 000 costs will be recovered
- **machine hour rate** – e.g. where machinery is heavily used, budgeted machine hours being 50 000 in the period, each hour that a machine is used will be charged at £6 (£300 000/50 000).

Costing methods

Examples of process costing industries include chemicals, distillation (e.g. petrol) and food.

There are two main categories: **specific order** costing – costs are charged directly to cost units – such as job, batch and contract costing, and **continuous operation** costing – costs have to be apportioned to cost units – such as service and process costing.

- **Job** costing is used when work is undertaken to a **customer's specific requirements**: all costs are charged to the job. **Contract** costing is similar, though the contract (e.g. for construction of a ship) tends to be for a longer duration.
- **Batch** costing is used when a **quantity of identical articles** (such as similar houses on an estate) are manufactured.

Key points from AS

- **Cost classifications and analysis**
  Revise AS pages 87–88

- Service (or **function**) costing is concerned with establishing the costs of services rendered, and controlling these costs (e.g. within a hospital).
- The **process** costing method is used when products are made **in a single process**.

> The costing method chosen must suit the manufacturing method.

KEY POINTS

Budgeting and forecasting

AQA A	AS
EDEXCEL	M4
OCR	M5
WJEC	M3
CCEA	M4

Efficient variance analysis requires accurate calculation and interpretation.

Management by exception

Budgeting helps **control** the finance available to a business. Budgetary control produces **variances** that allow managers to **compare the expected (budgeted) performance of their department with its actual performance**. These individual variances can be broken down into **sub-variances**. For example, a favourable sales variance might consist of a favourable **volume** variance – more are sold than had been planned – and an adverse **price** variance (the actual selling price is below the budgeted level, which may be the reason for the favourable volume variance).

Variances may be **controllable** by managers. In the above example the sales manager may have made a conscious decision to lower prices and increase sales volume, the product's price elasticity of demand leading to the increase in total revenue (the overall favourable variance). Other variances may be **non-controllable**, e.g. an adverse labour variance being due to a national wage agreement. Managers can only be held responsible for the variances they can control.

Flexing the budget

Budgets and variances must be adjusted for changes in volume. Comparing production budget figures based on an expected output of, say, 3000 units with the actual costs based on an actual output of 3500 units is not comparing like with like. The budget figures have to be **flexed** – scaled – accordingly, and these amended budget figures can then be compared accurately with the actual ones.

Setting standard costs is a more detailed and thorough process than establishing budgets, though budgeting estimates costs of all business areas (standard costing concentrates on products and services).

Standard costing

A 'standard cost' is a cost estimated by managers from information on expected prices and efficiency levels of production. Like budgets, standard costs provide **targets** for managers against which their individual performances can be appraised. It is linked with budgetary control: for example, it is easy to establish sales and production budgets once standard costs have been set.

There are three main variance groups in standard costing:

- **sales variances** – the sales **price** variance measures the difference between the standard and actual selling prices, and the sales **volume** variance measures the effect on profit of the difference between the actual and expected numbers sold
- **production cost variances** – total cost variances are calculated for **direct labour**, **direct materials** and **production overheads**, each being subdivided to show 'price' and 'quantity' sub-variances.

Key points from AS

- **Budgeting**
  Revise AS pages 84–85
- **Budgetary control**
  Revise AS pages 85–86
- **Cash flow forecasting**
  Revise AS pages 86–87

Direct labour:	
a **rate** variance based on the difference between actual and standard pay; an **efficiency** variance based on whether output is above or below standard.	*(standard – actual rate) × actual hours worked* *(standard – actual hours) × standard hourly rate*
Direct materials:	
a **price** variance based on the difference between actual and standard unit prices; a **usage** variance based on the difference between actual and standard quantities.	*(standard – actual price) × actual quantity* *(standard – actual quantity) × standard price*
Production overheads:	
variances based on differences between expected and actual volumes of use, efficiency and expenditure.	*Fixed overhead total variance, subdivided into* **expenditure** *(budgeted – actual expenditure) and* **volume** *([budgeted – actual volume] × unit absorption rate)*

> Management accounting draws on financial accounting information, but also involves detailed internal analyses through setting budgets and standard costs.
>
> **KEY POINTS**

Forecasting cash flow

Any forecast may be inaccurate: for example, any difference between budgeted and actual sales will affect cash inflows. Managers must therefore **monitor** the accuracy of the cash flow forecast. If it indicates that cash flow must be improved, the managers may:

- calculate and review the **cash cycle** (page 83)
- factor debtors, use **sale/leaseback** or examine other ways of **controlling working capital** (for example, by reducing stock levels).

> It is just as important to identify large cash surpluses as well as large cash deficits, to ensure surplus cash is used efficiently.
>
> **KEY POINTS**

Progress check

1 What is 'management by exception'?

2 State the main differences between standard costing and budgetary control.

3 What is the difference between apportionment and absorption?

1 Variances are calculated and the reasons for the variances are analysed.

2 Standard costing is more detailed, and is normally limited to products/services within the firm.

3 Apportionment: sharing the cost between more than one cost centre. Absorption: recovering overhead costs, e.g. through machine hours.

6.6 Contribution and marginal costing

After studying this section you should be able to:

- *calculate contribution, break-even and margin of safety*
- *apply this to decision-making using marginal costing principles*

LEARNING SUMMARY

Marginal costing and decision-making

AQA	M4
EDEXCEL	M4
OCR	M5
WJEC	M3
CCEA	M4

We know from AS that the difference between unit selling price and unit variable cost is the **contribution** made by the individual product towards the firm's fixed costs. When enough individual contributions have been made, the firm's total costs will be covered and it is at break-even point, making neither a profit nor a loss.

Contribution analysis therefore divides costs into their fixed and variable elements. Traditional **absorption** costing takes all costs into account when making decisions. A **marginal costing** approach can be used in decision-making, based on the argument that **factors having no bearing on a decision are ignored**. In this context, we ignore fixed costs on the argument that:

- they have to be paid regardless of income
- the apportionment of these fixed costs between different product lines is often arbitrary.

Examples of where a marginal costing approach is often used to make decisions include special orders, whether to discontinue a product, and 'make or buy' decisions.

Special orders

Here is an adapted A Level question where marginal costing and product contribution can be used to make a decision.

> A single-product manufacturer has this cost structure: materials £25, direct labour £28, and variable overheads £12 per unit; fixed overheads total £420 000. Its product price is £120, annual output (80% of capacity) being 20 000.
> A DIY store has enquired whether it can buy an extra 4000 units per annum, to sell as 'own label' items. It will pay £85 for each unit. The manufacturer will have to incur £10 000 set-up costs.
> Is the offer worth accepting?

The present contribution is £55 per product: selling price £120 less £65 variable costs (i.e. £25 + £28 + £12). Break-even point is £420 000/£55 = 7636 sales, the margin of safety is 12 364 (20 000 − 7636) and the forecast profit is £680 000 (12 364 × £55). Note how these calculations can be checked:

- break-even revenue £120 × 7636 = £916 320
- break-even costs total the same, i.e. £420 000 + £496 340 (7636 × £65) (the £20 difference is due to rounding)
- profit at 20 000 output = revenue £2 400 000 (£120 × 20 000) less cost £1 720 000 (£420 000 fixed + £1 300 000 variable, i.e. 20 000 × £65) = £680 000

Rounding of figures may mean slight differences in totals obtained.

The key question is: should the new order be taken on? Numerically, the calculations for this order show:

- unit contribution £20 (£85 − £65)
- total contribution £80 000 (4000 × £20)
- total profit £70 000 (£80 000 − £10 000 set-up costs).

Key points from AS

- **Break-even analysis** *Revise AS pages 88–89*

The main marginal costing principle here is that, **because all fixed costs are already covered** (by the normal production and sales exceeding the break-even point), **the contribution made by this special order is all profit**.

Non-financial factors are also important in making such decisions. For example:

- is the special order the most profitable way of utilising spare capacity, or will long-term plans for using this capacity be affected?
- will the lower selling price influence other customers?

> Extra contribution equals extra profit, once the break-even point has been reached.

Discontinuing products

Another area of decision-making involves whether to discontinue an apparently unprofitable product or line. For example:

A company makes three products, A, B and C. Costs are split one-third fixed and two-thirds variable. Figures are:

	A	B	C	Total
Sales (£000)	32	50	45	127
Total costs (£000)	36	39	33	108
Profit/(loss)	(4)	11	12	19

Should product A be dropped?

> Being indirect in nature, fixed costs may be shared arbitrarily between products.

Apparently, the overall profit of £19000 masks a loss of £4000 for product A. Since **fixed costs are apportioned without certainty**, we can remove them from the calculations and display the information as a **marginal costing statement**:

	A	B	C	Total
Sales	32	50	45	127
Variable costs	24	26	22	72
Contribution	8	24	23	55
Less fixed costs				36
Profit				19

Total profit remains the same, but by calculating individual product contributions we can see that **each product makes a contribution towards total fixed costs**. On this argument, therefore, product A should be retained.

> Marginal costing approaches take account of contribution made towards total fixed costs, and avoid the arbitrary apportionment of fixed (indirect) costs to individual products.

KEY POINTS

Progress check

1 How is break-even calculated?

2 What is the relationship between fixed costs, contribution and profit?

3 How does a marginal costing statement differ from a traditional cost statement?

1 Total fixed costs are divided by unit contribution.

2 Once total contribution covers fixed costs, further contribution = profit.

3 Costs are separated into fixed and variable, and contribution is calculated from which the fixed costs are deducted.

Sample questions and model answers

1

The accountant of a manufacturing firm has produced this information:

Balance Sheet (extract) as at 31 December 2001	£000	£000
Fixed Assets	1500	
Depreciation	300	1200
Current Assets:		
Stocks	300	
Debtors	150	
Cash	100	550
Current Liabilities:		
Creditors	150	
Corporation tax	300	450
Net Current Assets		100

The sales forecast for the first six months of 2002 (£000) is:

	Jan	Feb	Mar	Apr	May	Jun
Sales (£000)	120	600	600	120	120	120

These sales will be on one month's credit. The year-end debtors will have paid by the end of January. Raw materials will be bought (£90 000 per month) on two months' credit (year-end creditors will pay by the end of February). Other figures are £30 000 for operating expenses and £90 000 for wages, both paid in the month in which they are incurred. The tax owing will be paid in March.

(a) Prepare a monthly cash flow forecast for the first six months of 2002. [6]

(b) Comment on the results of your calculations. [4]

(c) How will depreciation affect your forecast? [2]

(a)

	Jan £000	Feb £000	Mar £000	Apr £000	May £000	Jun £000
Receipts from debtors	150	120	600	600	120	120
Payments:						
to creditors	75	75	90	90	90	90
for expenses	30	30	30	30	30	30
for wages	90	90	90	90	90	90
for tax			300			
Net cash inflow/(outflow)	(45)	(75)	90	390	(90)	(90)
Cash at start	100	55	(20)	70	460	370
Cash at close	55	(20)	70	460	370	280

> This is well laid out, and accurate. Using this format, the net cash flow can clearly be seen.

(b) The company has plenty of cash available, except at the end of February, when it will need to sort out an overdraft with its bank.

> An accurate assessment, but comments regarding (a) the large cash surpluses in the last three months, and (b) the gradually reducing total balance, should have been made.

(c) Depreciation isn't paid out in cash, so it won't show in the workings.

> A reasonable comment, though the phrase 'non-cash expense' would help make the explanation clearer.

Sample questions and model answers *(continued)*

2

Bentley Ltd produces kitchen scales that are sold to retailers for £10 each. Its expected output is 80 000 scales per annum, which is 80% of full capacity. Fixed costs have been calculated at £1.50 (based on full capacity), wage costs £1 per item, materials £4 per item and other variable costs £1 per item.

(a) Calculate the break-even level of output and the margin of safety [2]

The firm has received an offer from a major high-street chain to buy 20 000 scales at £6.50 each. These scales would feature a different plastic casing, and a machine costing £10 000 would need to be bought to make this casing.

(b) Should the company accept this offer? Evaluate both the numerical and non-numerical factors that should be taken into account. [8]

The answer is laid out clearly, though all calculations (e.g. how the variable cost total is arrived at, and the fixed cost calculation) should still be shown. The 'proof' of the break-even calculation should be calculated: it is

total revenue 37500 × £10
= £375000
total cost: variable 37500 × £6
= £225000
fixed = £150000
total = £375000

42500 is a more accurate statement of the margin of safety (it is better to use the actual output of 80000 rather than the maximum of 100000).

Accurate calculations again, though workings for total revenue (20000 × 50p) should still be displayed.

The analysis is lacking in detail, however: the candidate should consider points such as:

- all the spare capacity is now being used
- can the new machine be re-used?
- where will the £10000 required come from?
- is there a prospect of future orders?
- will the firm gain from publicity (is it an 'own label' order)?

(a) Contribution is £10 selling price less £6 variable costs = £4 per unit.

$$\text{Break-even point} = \frac{£150\,000 \text{ fixed costs}}{£4 \text{ contribution}} = 37\,500 \text{ units}$$

Margin of safety = 100 000 − 37 500 = 62 500 units

(b) Contribution for the new order = 50p per unit, £6.50 selling price less £6.00 variable costs. If the firm can sell 20 000, it will receive £10 000, but has had to pay out £10 000. It therefore makes neither a profit nor a loss, and breaks even on this order. I do not think it is a good idea, because no profit is made.

Practice examination questions

1 Leigh and Arthur are in business together, operating as a partnership and producing cuddly toys. They have been successful over the last five years, making large profits. They have decided to try and increase their output by obtaining new premises and machinery. They also plan to employ additional staff.

How could budgeting help Leigh and Arthur? [18]

2 Delphware plc is a large manufacturer of china and is quoted on the London Stock Exchange. The company is currently financed by £5m of Issued Share Capital in the form of ordinary shares and has sold debentures to the value of £1m. It also has a ten-year loan from the bank to the value of £0.5m. Delphware plc's Authorised Share Capital is £5m and total Capital Employed is £7.5m.

Delphware plc is facing increasing competition and recognises that it must modernise if it is going to compete effectively. It needs £900 000 to upgrade its plant and £100 000 for new machinery.

(i) Explain what is meant by the term 'gearing'. [2]

(ii) (a) Using the information above, calculate the gearing of Delphware plc in relation to its capital employed. [3]

(b) If you were a major shareholder in Delphware plc, would you be happy about the level of the firm's gearing? Explain your answer. [7]

(iii) Evaluate Delphware plc's decision to finance the upgrade of its plant through selling £900 000 of debentures and leasing its new machinery. [18]

CCEA 2000, GCE A Level, Business Studies, paper 1

Chapter 7

People in organisations

The following topics are covered in this chapter:

- Human resource planning
- Communication
- Employer–employee relations

- Trade unions
- Employment law

7.1 Human resource planning

LEARNING SUMMARY

After studying this section you should be able to:

- explain the importance of workforce planning
- identify and comment on key trends in the UK labour market
- describe and evaluate the importance of productivity to a firm

The labour market

AQA	M5
EDEXCEL	M5
OCR	M6
WJEC	M4
CCEA	M4

The importance of workforce planning

The firm will need an overall workforce (or human resource) strategy. In achieving this, HRM will need to work closely with other departments to ensure the firm is employing people with the **right skills** at the **right time**.

The workforce plan contains an assessment of:

- national and local changes in the population, analysed by **numbers**, **ages**, **skills** and **location**
- an analysis of the current **internal labour supply**
- consideration of any proposed developments in the company's **organisation**, **location** and **structure**.

> The workforce plan therefore depends on **external** and **internal** analysis.

This information can be used to evaluate the likely effects on labour turnover, the implications for **recruitment**, expected **training** requirements for existing and anticipated new staff, and the probable effects on **morale** and **labour relations**.

The main difficulty of creating a workforce plan is the problem of **estimating future demand** for labour. Demand will change as a result of the firm changing strategy (e.g. new markets opening up, existing market demand falling), and competitor actions.

Many organisations adopt a '**core and periphery**' approach, employing a core of highly trained full-time staff, which is supplemented by a periphery of part-time – often temporary – employees. This can bring greater staffing flexibility, although part-time staff may lack motivation, and communication becomes more difficult.

> **KEY POINTS**
>
> HRM emphasises that **people** are an organisation's key resource due to their flexibility, creativity and commitment.

Key points from AS

- **Workforce planning**
  Revise AS pages 93–95

Trends in the labour market

New working patterns and arrangements include the growth in part-time work, and increased numbers of women in the UK workforce.

1 Changes in **full-time** and **part-time** employment

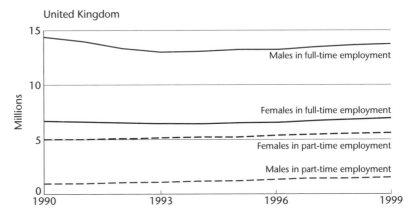

Figure 7.1 *Full and part-time employment*   Source: ONS

2 Changes in **household/family size**

	Percentages	
	1981	**1999**
One person in household, under pensionable age	8	14
Couple with no children	26	30
Couple with dependent children	31	23
Lone parent with dependent children	5	7

Source: ONS

3 Changes in **age** of the labour force

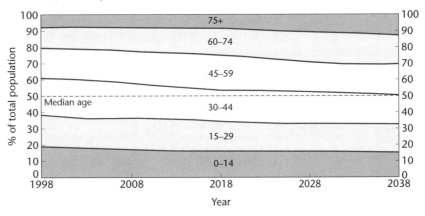

Figure 7.2 *Projected age distribution, UK 1998–2038*   Source: ONS

4 Changes in **employment status**

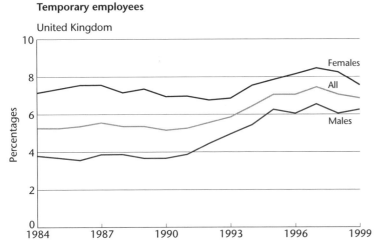

Figure 7.3 *Changes in employment*   Source: ONS

5 Changes in **working patterns**

	Percentages (Spring 1999)		
	Males	*Females*	*All employees*
Full-time employees			
Flexible working hours	8.4	13.3	10.2
Other flexible working patterns (e.g. term-time working only)	7.1	12.2	8.1
Total	*15.5*	*23.5*	*18.3*
Part-time employees			
Flexible working hours	5.9	8.1	7.7
Other flexible working patterns (e.g. term-time working only)	9.2	16.1	14.9
Total	*15.1*	*24.2*	*22.6*

The effect of these changes on the workforce plan

> For the **employee**, part-time and flexible work may suit family needs, but also makes it more difficult to plan/budget for the longer term.

There is a more **flexible** and **cheaper** labour force, but firms must now provide the same conditions of employment as for full-time staff. An ageing workforce may result in greater **absenteeism** (through illness), may prove **less flexible**, and may need **further retraining** to update skills.

Many firms adopt 'family-friendly' or 'work–life balance' policies, such as job-sharing and shift-swap (e.g. at Asda) in order that they can accommodate people, mainly women, with young families in their workforce plan. Measures to improve work–life balance are seen as important, and can improve attendance and productivity: for example, in 1999 Barclays Bank discovered that job-sharing teams had much better sickness records than equivalent full-time teams.

> Changing working patterns can make **communication** more difficult for both parties, e.g. with part-time employees, and full-time staff working from home.
>
> **KEY POINTS**

Productivity

AQA	M5
EDEXCEL	M5
OCR	M6
WJEC	M4
CCEA	M4

> Other influences on competitiveness include product design and quality, and the efficiency of other functional areas (especially marketing).

Labour productivity

One way of avoiding recruiting additional staff is to get more from the existing workforce. Although HRM argues that, to the organisation, people are **an asset rather than a cost** to be controlled, management will be concerned with improving the workforce's **cost-effectiveness**, which they do by measuring its productivity. 'Productivity' can be defined as **measuring outputs in relation to inputs**. It is an important determinant of a firm's national and international competitiveness: the more productive the firm is, the lower its unit costs and the more price-competitive it will be.

Labour productivity is calculated as follows:

$$\frac{output\ per\ period}{number\ of\ employees}$$

It measures **employee efficiency** the level of this efficiency depends on individual employees, but is also influenced by the following.

- The level of employee **motivation** – e.g. acknowledging the importance of motivators as well as hygiene factors will improve motivation, and the more efficient the organisation's communication system is, the more motivated and productive the staff will be.
- The amount and quality of staff **training** – many firms acknowledge the value of investing in staff training, e.g. the increase in product quality and reduction of the percentage of rejects.

The short-term emphasis may be to increase production rather than productivity (which is a longer-term goal).

- The **equipment** being used – investing in more modern machinery can improve output and thereby increase productivity; it may also be possible to use existing equipment more efficiently.
- The firm's **culture** – for example, adopting the **kaizen** approach to continuous improvement is associated with increases in productivity.

There are three related indicators of a firm's productivity.

- **Labour turnover** – LTO will alter according to how staff react to any changed production methods and new equipment introduced to improve productivity.
- **Health and safety** – changes in this performance indicator may reflect how staff have accepted and reacted to the new work practices.
- **Absenteeism** – staff may miss work due to **non-avoidable** factors such as illness; others miss work because of **avoidable** factors, e.g. because there is a lack of Herzberg's hygiene factors present.

The costs of high LTO, a poor health and safety record, and high levels of absenteeism include having to employ staff for extra hours (often on overtime rates) to make up production, and being forced to prioritise work whenever there is not enough available labour.

Problems of improving productivity

There can also be a reluctance to accept any form of change... in this context, changes in working practices.

Managers may face difficulties increasing productivity as a result of **shortage of resources** (mainly shortage of funds). They may also experience **problems in persuading employees**. Even though productivity improvements are often linked with pay, many staff may fear that an increase in productivity will lead to a loss of jobs. However, if managers fail to increase productivity they may find the firm becomes uncompetitive, with the need for major job losses and restructuring.

> The faster productivity grows, the less need there will be to appoint new staff, thus saving substantial costs.

KEY POINTS

Progress check

1 Why do companies undertake human resource planning?
2 How is labour productivity calculated?

2 Output divided by number of employees.

1 To ensure the right people with the right skills are employed at the right time.

7.2 Communication

LEARNING SUMMARY

After studying this section you should be able to:

- outline the importance of effective communication to an organisation
- explain and illustrate the meaning of 'communication networks'
- examine the relationship between communication and motivation

The importance of efficient communication

AQA	M5
EDEXCEL	AS
OCR	M6
WJEC	M4
CCEA	M4

> For communication to be classed as efficient, the information transmitted must be **easily accessible** to the recipient, and sent in a **cost-effective** way.

Communication takes place within the organisation, and with outside agencies. **Internal** communication may flow down the hierarchy through the chain of command, or may be more informal. **External** communication tends to be more formal, taking place with the major external stakeholders: suppliers, customers, shareholders, the government and the public.

The **purpose** of the communication varies, as shown in figure 7.4. An influence on which medium is selected will be whether the communication is primarily **one-way** or **two-way**.

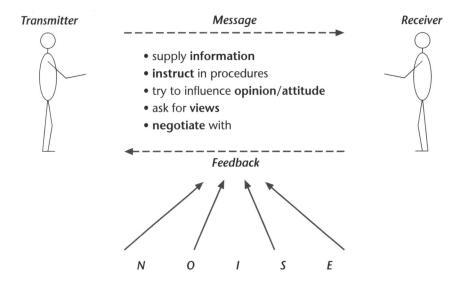

Figure 7.4 Communication

Communication networks

> Flatter structures with wider spans of control often allow employees greater personal autonomy and control.

All communication takes place within **formal** or **informal** networks. Formal networks are closely associated with the organisation's structure, e.g. as shown on the organisation chart. The chart shows the formal communication through the lines of **authority**, and the relationship between the various departments or functions.

A formal, 'chain' network is based on the existing **chains of command** within the organisation. Communications are transmitted from superior to subordinate along the chain. This network is therefore associated with **tall structures** and **authoritarian** organisations.

> **Key points from AS**
>
> - **Role of business communication**
>   *Revise AS pages 50–51*
> - **Barriers to effective communication**
>   *Revise AS page 51*
> - **Features of organisational structure**
>   *Revise AS pages 47–49*

A different communication network is the **matrix** (or 'all-channel') network. Here, every member of the matrix group communicates with each other, often without there being a formal leader. Alternatives include the **horizontal** or 'circular' communication channel, e.g. when team members communicate with each other at team meetings, and the **wheel** or 'hub' channel, where there is central control (e.g. head office).

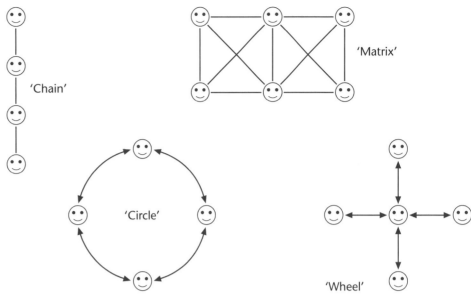

Figure 7.5 *Different communication networks*

Informal channels assume greater importance when the formal networks are not working efficiently.

Communication and motivation

There is a close relationship between communication and motivation. An example is in the range of informal networks that coexist with the formal ones. **Human needs** – e.g. for contact, friendship and recognition – help in creating these informal channels.

The main characteristics of an informal network are the **fast transmission** and the **variable accuracy** of the information. The **quality** of the communication will therefore vary, being influenced by the (subjective) judgement of those transmitting the information.

Managers need to recognise the importance of good formal and informal communication in the organisation. To motivate employees, they need to communicate:

Staff appraisal schemes are often used to communicate employee levels of achievement.

- the organisation's mission statement and strategic **objectives**
- its **performance** in the market-place
- the **relevance** of the employees' work to the achievement of objectives and market performance
- how **effective** the employee is in relation to this.

By doing so they will motivate staff, e.g. in Maslow's terms by improving their self-esteem and achieving levels of self-actualisation.

The influence of size

The larger the firm, the more layers there tend to be in the organisational structure. As a result, communication slows down and becomes over-formalised. In turn, this slows down decision-making, and can have a negative effect on staff morale. 'Noise' also increases, with the message more likely to be distorted as a result of going through more levels (i.e. more people).

The way that many large organisations have to cope with the volume of communication required is to commit it to a written form (including email). As a result, there can be '**communication overload**', with staff having to **prioritise** communications (sometimes without having the information to make this judgement), or even completely ignoring the communication.

Although Information Communications Technology (ICT) is used to overcome the slowness of communication in large companies, it can also create a much greater volume of communication.

7.3 Employer–employee relations

After studying this section you should be able to:

- *explain the importance of motivating employees*
- *evaluate the main ways firms use to motivate employees*
- *analyse the value of employee participation.*

LEARNING SUMMARY

Motivating the workforce

AQA	M5
EDEXCEL	M5
OCR	M6
WJEC	M4
CCEA	M4

HRM's 'hard' model concentrates more on assessing the firm's staffing needs quantitatively rather than qualitatively.

The 'soft' model of HRM emphasises a motivational, **humanistic** approach to labour relations, e.g. by encouraging employee **involvement**.

Involving staff

Managers may try to motivate staff using individual and group-based approaches.

Job rotation provides staff with a range of different work activities. It is easy to plan, although staff will require additional training to carry out unfamiliar tasks. Job rotation works most efficiently when the tasks being rotated require similar skills, and are at similar levels of difficulty.

Maslow's social needs illustrate the value of group approaches.

Job enrichment incorporates job rotation but also provides the opportunity for employees to undertake **additional work with additional responsibility**. As a result, it is more time-consuming and costly to implement than job rotation, but provides greater levels of motivation through greater involvement.

Encouraging **teamwork** brings the benefits to individuals associated with working in groups: managers also gain from greater employee flexibility, e.g. the ability and willingness of group members to cover for absent staff.

Management by objectives (MBO)

Managers can use MBO as a **motivational** tool. MBO is based on objectives being agreed between a manager and subordinates.

MBO must be distinguished from management by **exception**, used for example in budgetary control.

- Targets are set for staff at all levels to achieve: these targets are **'personalised'** because the subordinates have been involved in setting them and, as a result, employees are encouraged to take **responsibility** for their actions.
- MBO **co-ordinates** effort through encouraging staff to work towards agreed common goals.
- The set targets provide an element of **control**, allowing performance to be judged against target.

Weaknesses of MBO as a motivational approach are that it can be **time-consuming**, and encourages **easily achieved targets** to be set.

Remunerating staff

Time-based or piece-based payment systems are often supported nowadays by **participation-based** payment schemes.

- **Performance-related pay** (PRP) schemes reward staff according to the quality of their work – individual targets are set, and staff exceeding these targets receive a higher-than-average payment. The PRP approach is increasingly criticised on the grounds that it can be **divisive**, e.g. when it focuses on the individual rather than the group, or when there is a belief that some employees receive PRP not on merit but due to favouritism.
- **Share ownership** schemes may be in a 'save as you earn' (**SAYE**) format, where staff can save with an option to use these savings to buy shares at a set

Key points from AS

- **Motivation**
  Revise AS pages 101–103

rate (often based on the share price when the scheme was offered), or 'share option' formats, managers being given an option to buy shares at favourable rates. Both formats attempt to enhance motivation through staff having a greater stake in the success of the company.

- **Profit-sharing** schemes reward staff with a share of the firm's profits. These schemes again encourage staff to identify with the firm's success.

'The Group operates three types of share option scheme: a worldwide scheme for all employees where legislation permits, a savings-related scheme for all UK employees and senior executives' schemes in the UK and overseas.'

Pilkington plc, directors' report and accounts, 2000

'Staff entitled to participate in the Group's profit sharing schemes will receive a profit share of 10% of basic salaries as at 30 September 1999. The total payment to be made will be £47 million (1998 – £43 million).'

Royal Bank of Scotland Group plc, chairman's statement, 1999

'In August 1999, we introduced a new scheme offering share options to all 111,000 eligible UK colleagues with one financial year's service who did not otherwise participate in our executive schemes. In December 1999, the Company received a prestigious ProShare award for "Employee Participation and Involvement" for its employee share schemes.'

J Sainsbury plc annual report and accounts, 2000

Figure 7.6 Examples of profit-sharing and share option schemes

> Other participation-based schemes, e.g. bonus and suggestion schemes, also illustrate 'reward management' practices.

In late 1999, research was conducted by William M. Mercer and the City University Business School into the impact of all-employee share plans on the productivity of 250 companies. The research suggests that those companies adopting the SAYE scheme in particular are outpacing other companies in terms of **productivity**, where there was a high level of employee participation in these schemes. Productivity improved by 3% in these companies. In addition, certain human resource practices that complemented the share plan, such as employee participation in decision-making, produced up to an additional 3% productivity. This compared with 'Company Share Option Plan' schemes and 'Approved Profit Sharing' schemes, where no effect on productivity was noted: these schemes simply functioned as **rewards** for employees.

> These additional forms of remuneration can motivate staff, although – since no one employee can have a significant effect on profit performance – they may not always have a substantial incentive effect.
>
> **KEY POINTS**

The impact of the minimum wage

As a result of the **Minimum Wage Act** 1998, from April 1999 the UK now has a minimum wage in line with the rest of the EU and many other advanced economies. The argument advanced for the minimum wage was to provide a reasonable return for all employees, which would give additional motivation as well as lift some of them out of the 'poverty trap'. The argument against this was that employers' wage costs would rise and therefore increase prices and affect competitiveness.

> Employment statistics and other evidence indicates that the UK economy has not been adversely affected by the minimum wage.
>
> **KEY POINTS**

Employee participation and industrial democracy

AQA	M5
EDEXCEL	M4
OCR	M6
WJEC	M4
CCEA	M4

Participation

The main ways staff participate directly are through **quality circles, works councils** and being appointed as **worker directors**. There is also increasing participation through creating **employee shareholders** and introducing **profit-sharing schemes**.

Although the value of involving employees in discussions and decision-making is recognised by many theorists, problems can also arise through employee participation.

Employees may also have increased expectations of even greater involvement, which may conflict with the firm's policy.

- There can be a **slowing** of decision-making.
- **Cost** (e.g. attendance at meetings rather than active involvement in production) increases.
- **Resentment** by managers of employee involvement may exist.

External influences

The **UK government** sees its role as 'to promote partnership between employers and employees', through 'the sharing of information and increased consultation' (1999).

Trade unions may also make a positive contribution to employee participation and communication.

- Unions act as a **communication channel**, through which management can communicate with employees.
- They encourage **collective bargaining** to take place, removing the need to reach an agreement with every member of staff individually.
- They **participate** with management in decision-making, e.g. on retraining staff.
- Unions are **consulted** regarding major decisions, and relay the results of this consultation to their members.

Progress check

1 Identify **three** different types of communication networks.
2 Explain the difference between job rotation and job enrichment.
3 What participation-based remuneration schemes are available?

3 Profit-sharing; share ownership; performance-related pay.
2 Job rotation provides extra activities; job enrichment does this, but also includes extra responsibility.
1 Chain; matrix; wheel.

7.4 Trade unions

After studying this section you should be able to:

- outline the types, function and aims of trade unions
- explain the typical benefits to members arising from union membership
- analyse the various forms of industrial action, and outline the role of ACAS in settling such action

Types and functions

AQA	M5
EDEXCEL	M4
OCR	M6
WJEC	M4
CCEA	M4

Unlike a company's own staff association, a trade union is an **independent** organisation.

Why do people join unions? These reasons are normally given, in order of importance *(source, British Social Attitude Survey)*:

- to protect **jobs**
- to improve **working conditions**
- to improve **pay**
- to have **more say** over management's long-term plans.

Type	Nature	Features	Examples (membership in 2000)
Craft	Originally set up to control entrants to particular skilled occupations.	Often very small, and one company may find a number of them representing its workforce, making negotiations difficult.	The Musicians' Union (MU) with 30 000 members, and CATU, the Ceramic and Allied Trades Union with 19 000 members.
Industrial	Contains most of the workers in an industry.	Managers tend to find negotiations are more straightforward through dealing with only one union.	The retail trade's USDAW (Union of Shop, Distributive and Allied Workers), with about 300 000 members.
General	Often very large, may contain high proportions of semi-skilled and unskilled workers from different industries.	The large size of the union and the wide range of interests it represents can create difficulties for the union.	UNISON, about $1\frac{1}{4}$ million members, is a general union for public sector employees, e.g. in local government, health care, power supply and transport.
White-collar	Contains clerical and professional staff.	Often 'industrial', containing members from a single white-collar occupation.	National Union of Teachers, with about 200 000 members.

These trade unions are normally structured as shown in figure 7.7

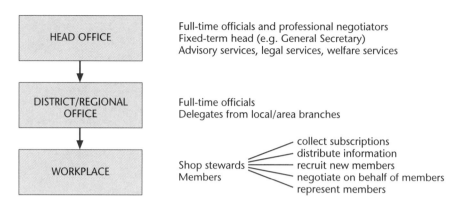

Figure 7.7 Trade union structure

Three important trends have been for:

> Many small unions still exist: e.g. in 2000, the Professional Footballers Association (2200 members), and Sheffield Wool Shear Workers Union (10 members).

1 **union membership to fall**, both in total (from about 13 million in 1979 to about 8 million in 2000) and as a percentage of the UK's workforce – reasons include increased numbers of temporary or part-time jobs (these employees being less likely to join unions), and fewer manufacturing-based jobs, where union membership was traditionally very high

2 unions to **merge and grow in size** – about two-thirds of union members belong to the ten largest unions

3 unions to negotiate **single-union agreements**, which from management's view can help negotiation and may effectively rule out strike action.

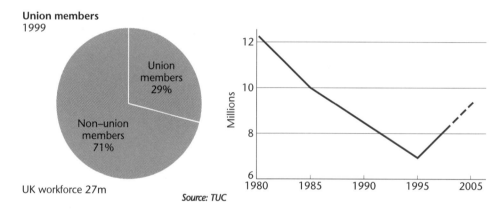

	Percentages			
	1992		**1998**	
	males	*females*	*males*	*females*
Managers and administrators	24	24	18	21
Professional	44	62	39	62
Clerical and secretarial	41	27	30	22
Selling	16	13	8	12
Craft and related	45	34	33	28
Other occupations	41	26	32	21
All occupations	40	32	31	28

Figure 7.8 Figures on UK trade union membership

Source: ONS

Union activity

A trade union undertakes a range of activities.

> Unions win over £300 million each year as compensation for members who suffer injuries, or discrimination at work.

- It **advises, represents and protects** members:
  - it advises on procedures following industrial accidents, represents employees at industrial tribunals, and gives general legal advice

- it ensures members receive sick pay and other benefits to which they are entitled
- it helps protect against redundancy, unfair dismissal, disciplinary action and discrimination.
- **It negotiates** with employers for:
  - improved pay and conditions
  - greater job satisfaction and better job security
  - improved pension and retirement arrangements.
- It **seeks to influence others:**
  - as a pressure group influencing employers and governments on legislation and other matters
  - regarding social objectives such as full employment and better social security arrangements.

Many members see **collective bargaining** as the most important function of their union. The two main methods of collective bargaining are:

- **integrative** bargaining, where both sides seek to negotiate a pay and productivity deal
- **distributive** bargaining, where each side negotiates from its exclusive standpoint.

> **KEY POINTS**
>
> The main aim of a trade union is to improve the working life of its members.

The employer equivalent of the TUC is the **Confederation of British Industry** (CBI), representing a cross-section of companies in the UK economy.

Since unions have similar goals and mutual concerns, it is in their collective interest to come together and agree common policies and approaches. The **Trades Union Congress** (TUC) acts as a central body and the collective voice of its affiliated unions. It promotes the general aims of the union movement and – like individual unions – acts as a pressure group to influence government policy.

Benefits of union membership

Union membership brings a number of benefits to its members, summarised in figure 7.9.

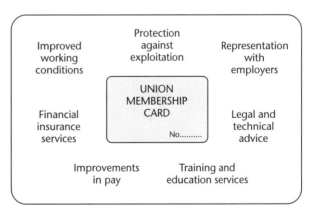

Figure 7.9 Benefits of union membership

Industrial disputes

Recently there has been greater government support for the union movement, e.g. allowing union recognition in a firm if the majority of staff request it.

Trade union power came under attack from the government in the 1980s. The **Employment Acts** passed between 1980 and 1990:

- required **secret ballots** to elect the main union officers, and for strike action
- protected individual members from disciplinary action for refusing to take part in a strike
- made secondary (i.e. indirect) industrial action illegal.

In recent years, days lost to industrial disputes have fallen, but collective bargaining doesn't always succeed, and disputes still occur.

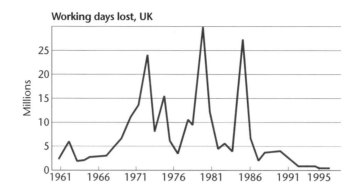

Days lost per 1000 employees		
1996	1997	1998
57	10	12

Figure 7.10 Working days lost to labour disputes.

Source: ONS

A union may take different forms of industrial action.

- With **overtime bans**, the union instructs its members not to work overtime: this leads to falling output and puts pressure on the employer to agree to the union's demands.
- In a **work-to-rule**, employees follow the 'rule book' very closely, which can slow down or even halt production.
- A **go-slow** occurs when members carry out their work more slowly than normal: this also reduces output.
- Employees may resort to **sit-ins**, refusing to leave the premises and occupying them in an attempt to make sure that goods neither enter nor leave the firm. Most sit-ins take place when there is a threat to close the business.

Finally, union members may go on strike and **withdraw their labour**. The losses to the economy as a whole include unemployed factors of production, lost output, less consumer choice, reduced tax revenue, and the possibility of increased imports and greater overseas involvement in the UK economy.

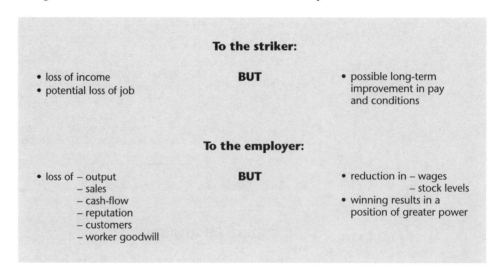

Unions normally regard strike action as a 'last resort' activity.

KEY POINTS

The role of ACAS

If the dispute carries on for some time, **ACAS** – the Advisory, Conciliation and Arbitration Service – may become involved. ACAS was set up in 1975 to improve industrial relations. It is independent from both employers and unions, and offers these main services.

- **Conciliation.** An ACAS official discusses the dispute with both parties to find areas of common ground, which might form the basis for further negotiations.
- **Arbitration.** If both sides agree, their dispute 'goes to arbitration'. ACAS provides an independent third party to listen to the points made, and offers a settlement (the employer and the union, by going to arbitration, have agreed to accept whatever settlement is offered). If 'pendulum' arbitration is used, the arbitrator makes a straight choice between the two sides (this discourages either party from taking an unrealistic bargaining position).
- **Mediation.** The ACAS official suggests a solution to the dispute, which is then considered by the parties.

Other ACAS services include publishing guidelines and codes of practice on industrial relations.

'To improve the performance and effectiveness of organisations by providing an independent and impartial service to prevent and resolve disputes and to build harmonious relationships at work.'

Figure 7.11 *The mission statement of ACAS*

Progress check

1 State the main aim of a trade union.
2 Name **four** forms of industrial action other than strike action.

2 Overtime ban; work-to-rule; go-slow; sit-in.

1 To improve the working life of members.

7.5 Employment law

After studying this section you should be able to:

- *summarise the main legal influences on employment*
- *explain and illustrate the influence of the EU on employment law*

Principles of employment law

AQA	M5
EDEXCEL	M4
OCR	M6
WJEC	M4
CCEA	M4

> Modern UK legislation often uses the term 'workers' rather than 'employees' when there is a need to include self-employed people within the scope of the law.

In the UK, employees are protected against discrimination through equal pay, race, sex and disability discrimination laws. They are also protected against disclosure of personal information: the **Data Protection Act** 1998 protects staff from disclosure of information in areas such as recruitment, employment records, discipline and dismissal. It also deals with the issue of **employee monitoring**, e.g. as regards using email or accessing the Internet for personal use.

This legislation is supported by a range of EU Directives, many of which led to the UK laws being passed.

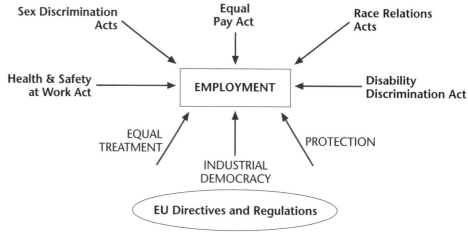

Figure 7.12 Legal influences on employment

Influence of the EU

The EU's main influence has been to:

- **support equal treatment** in the workplace
- **protect employees** from exploitation, and
- encourage **greater industrial democracy**.

> According to the Equal Opportunities Commission (1999), the UK ranks only tenth in the EU on equality of pay.

EU law supports UK law. For example, there is a 1975 EU Directive on equal pay for men and women which established, for work to which equal value is given, the principle of non-discrimination on the basis of pay.

The EU has influenced recent UK legislation such as the **Employment Regulations Act** 1999, which contains parental leave and similar provisions, and the **Working Time Regulations 1999**. Its 1989 **Community Charter of the Fundamental Social Rights of Workers** – the 'Social Charter' – establishes the general principles on which the EU model of labour law and the place of work in society is based. Its 'Social Chapter', to which the UK has now signed up, incorporates these principles and includes:

> **Key points from AS**
>
> - **Legislation at work**
>   *Revise AS pages 98–100*
> - **The EU**
>   *Revise AS page 67*

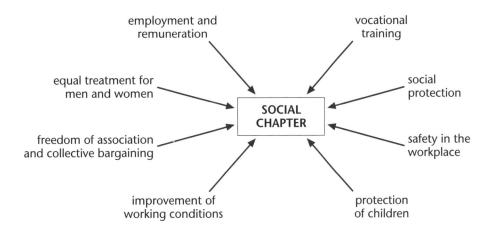

Figure 7.13 *Scope of the 'Social Chapter'*

Examples of EU influence

The **European Works Council Directive**, adopted in 1994, requires works councils for informing and consulting employees to be set up in companies employing over 1000 and which have bases with at least 150 workers in at least two member states. The company sets up a European Works Council or alternative voluntary consultation arrangements, which seek to inform and consult employees on key organisational issues such as the company's structure and proposed changes, employment, and health and safety matters.

> Management can withhold 'sensitive information' which, if revealed, would 'seriously harm the functioning of the undertaking concerned'. They can also require members of the Council to treat certain information as confidential.

The **Human Rights Act** 1998 came into force in the UK in October 2000. This Act will affect business in a number of ways: for example, it grants companies many of the same rights as individuals will have, and it imposes certain obligations on public authorities. The Act's provisions most likely to affect business are **Article 8** (the right to respect for privacy and family life), and **Articles 9 and 10**, which cover the freedom of thought and expression. Article 8 may mean employees have a right to privacy in relation to telephone calls made and emails sent. Article 10 will influence certain sectors such as the media industry, and may even allow employees to express views that clash with the employer's management of the workplace.

The **Working Time Directive** seeks to ensure that all workers enjoy satisfactory working conditions.

For example:

- **Article 3** a minimum daily rest period of 11 consecutive hours per 24-hour period
- **Article 4** a rest break if the working day is longer than six hours
- **Article 5** a minimum rest period of 24 hours (plus the 11 hours' daily rest period) in each seven-day period
- **Article 6** the average working time for each seven-day period, including overtime, does not exceed 48 hours
- **Article 7** annual paid leave of at least four weeks.

Other examples of EU legislation include:

- the **Posted Workers Directive** – this protects staff who are assigned to work in another EU member state by guaranteeing them certain minimum terms and conditions of employment, to ensure fair competition and prevent employers from undercutting local wages
- the **Part-Time Work Directive**, which provides for the equal treatment of part-time employees with full-time staff
- the **Parental Leave Directive**, allowing workers to take at least three months' unpaid leave following the birth or adoption of a child.

Employers must take this legislation into account. Larger companies can employ specialist legal staff: in smaller organisations, an employee such as the Company Secretary may be responsible for assessing the effect of the various laws on the business.

> UK and EU employment legislation both **supports** (e.g. by creating a 'level playing field' in employment and pay), and **constrains** business.

KEY POINTS

Progress check

1 In what ways does EU employment legislation influence business?

2 What are the main forms of employee protection?

1 It supports equal treatment in the workplace; it protects employees; it encourages participation and industrial democracy.

2 Against discrimination on the grounds of race, sex or disability; against disclosure of personal information; against unfair or unreasonable working conditions.

Sample question and model answer

1

Read the following newspaper report on the achievement of a local firm.

> **Local firm receives award**
>
> Salopian Ltd has won this year's '*Wrekin Read*' Best Employer award. The company employs 185 full-time and 70 part-time staff, and – despite facing problems in filling its order books – it has managed to retain its 'no redundancy' policy.
>
> The Human Resource Director at Salopian is Natalie Osborne. Born in the Wrekin area, Natalie joined Salopian two years ago. Soon afterwards, she introduced a staff appraisal scheme for all employees (including managers), and has implemented a policy of promoting from within. The company has an excellent safety record. It offers profit-related bonuses and a non-contributory pension scheme to all staff, and has recently implemented a Single Union agreement in the expectation that this will lead to even more flexible working practices.
>
> Natalie is particularly proud of innovations she has introduced to improve quality. All employees attend weekly quality circle meetings, discussing issues such as the working environment. Evidence of success here is in the company's growing productivity.

(a) Explain the possible benefits to Salopian from employing both full-time and part-time staff. [6]

(b) Examine the benefits to staff from having a Single Union agreement. [6]

(c) Evaluate the extent to which working practices at Salopian reflect the ideas of motivational theorists. [8]

This is a good analysis of employing part-time staff, but is not a balanced answer. It should outline the features of employing full-time staff, and reach some conclusion. Advantages of employing full-time staff include greater continuity and known stability, future planning is helped by knowing skill levels, productivity increases with greater commitment and loyalty, and there are lower personnel-based costs and more efficient channels of communication. A good conclusion is that the company should employ an appropriate 'mix' of full-time and part-time employees, to suit its short-term and long-term goals.

(a) I would recommend Salopian employs more part-time staff. By doing so, Salopian may be able to save money because the wage bill will be lower. This is because the company can monitor hours worked and therefore control labour costs. Although it can be difficult to communicate with, and monitor the work quality of, part-timers, Salopian will have a more flexible workforce able to respond more quickly to changing market conditions. It can also vary the skill levels employed more easily.

A good answer, though mention that there is greater consistency for both parties with a single negotiating and organising voice.

(b) The advantages to employees from a single union policy are that negotiations become more efficient, and that demarcation disputes shouldn't arise. The disadvantages are that there is a lack of recognition for members of other unions, and the possibility that the local branch will become subject to control by one group of employees who have their own interests.

A good effort to a difficult question. When you mention theorists by name, always try to refer to their theories: dealing with the above references, we could add: (1) Maslow's feeling of worth, and Herzberg's motivators (e.g. recognition and responsibility) and hygiene factor of security; (2) Mayo, interest in employees stimulates production; (3) Maslow, esteem and self-actualisation; (4) McGregor, Theory Y workers exercise their own control and direction.

(c) What we know from the article is that the company has a no redundancy policy, which will improve morale and motivation (Maslow and Herzberg[1]). It also has annual appraisal schemes (Mayo[2]). A policy like internal promotion would be supported by Maslow[3], and it is an example of Herzberg's motivators. There is evidence of flexible work practices (McGregor[4]), and the profit-related bonuses and non-contributory pension scheme are examples of satisfying Maslow's lower-order basic needs. Finally, the excellent safety record illustrates how the company takes account of Maslow's safety needs and Herzberg's hygiene factors of working conditions.

Practice examination questions

1 'It is good to see that over 70 000 of our staff are now shareholders and 106 000 are eligible for profit sharing this year' (Tesco plc annual review).

Critically appraise the value of employee shareholder and profit-sharing schemes to companies such as Tesco. [12]

2 According to a number of recent reports, the United Kingdom is on the brink of a 'workstyle revolution', with the traditional 'nine to five' working week gradually disappearing and being replaced by **flexible working**. As a result of these changes, many businesses report increased employee performance and satisfaction.

However, not all firms can accommodate these changes without disputes occurring. Employees unsettled by the process of change at the work-place may – especially if working in a unionised organisation – resort to using the organisation's grievance procedure.

(a) Suggest why flexible working may prove beneficial for
  (i)   the employer
  (ii) the employee. [6]

(b) How will union membership help employees who wish to follow a grievance procedure against their employers? [6]

Chapter 8

Operations management

The following topics are covered in this chapter:

- *Locating operations*
- *Developing operations*
- *Ensuring operational efficiency*

8.1 Locating operations

After studying this section you should be able to:

- *identify and describe the main factors determining where operations are located*
- *analyse how these are used in deciding where a firm is to be located*

LEARNING SUMMARY

The importance of location

AQA	M5
EDEXCEL	M4
OCR	M7, M10
WJEC	M5
CCEA	M5

An organisation combines the various factors of production as efficiently as possible, to produce its goods and services and sell them at a profit. The lower it can keep its unit costs, the greater its potential profit. The eventual choice of location is based on a **compromise** between various influences.

Key points from AS

- **External economies of scale**
  Revise AS page 57
- **Implementing a regional policy**
  Revise AS page 66
- **The European Union**
  Revise AS page 67
- **Social influences**
  Revise AS pages 71–72
- **Human resource planning**
  Revise AS pages 93–95

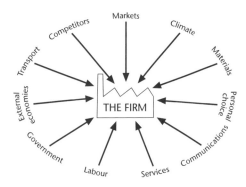

Figure 8.1 Influences on location

Historical and natural influences

A significant historical influence on location was the availability of **power**: for example, water power, coupled with a suitable climate, encouraged the location of the old staple industries of cotton and wool weaving in the north of England.

The **agricultural industry** has always been influenced by the suitability of local climatic and soil conditions. Other physical advantages such as good natural harbours near to areas of high population influenced industries such as shipbuilding to locate in, and contribute to the growth of, cities like Belfast and Sunderland. The topography and situation of the land can also influence location: for example, a chemical factory complex may need a large flat area of land near the coast.

Transport and communications

Cities like Birmingham and Manchester publicise the fact that their airports are becoming more important internationally.

Location near to an efficient transport network has become an increasingly important influence. Many firms now examine closely the **road and air links,** for both their raw materials and their finished products. Good transport systems are also required for the firm's labour.

Although the UK has national postal and telecommunications services, some 'high-tech' firms choose to locate in areas that offer more **advanced technological support** (e.g. where there are advanced cable technology systems available).

Labour

The availability of a sufficiently large and well-trained labour force is an influence although the move by some firms towards a more capital-intensive production, coupled with a greater willingness by staff to commute, can reduce the importance of this influence. When relocating, a firm may offer a range of financial inducements to encourage its workforce to move with it, due to the geographical immobility of labour: the alternative is to meet increased training costs. The availability of suitably skilled **managers** is a related influence.

> The firm has to examine the availability of suitable **quality** (skills) as well as suitable **quantity** of staff.

The **cost** of labour, as well as its availability, varies from area to area. If the firm is labour-intensive, it might be tempted to move to an area of the country with relatively low wage costs.

Materials and markets

Firms involved in 'weight-gaining' production, where the end product is heavier or bulkier than the inputs (for instance, the brewing industry), have traditionally located close to their markets. Those firms using 'weight-reducing' production processes – e.g. sugar refining, sawmills – and having bulky raw materials (and therefore high transport costs) have tended to locate near to the supply of these materials.

Many industries located where there was a concentrated supply of their raw materials nearby: examples include the china industry in and around Stoke-on-Trent, and Sheffield's steel industry. Now that these firms have to import their raw materials from abroad, newer firms in the industry may choose to locate elsewhere, although the existence of **external economies** and '**industrial inertia**' still encourage them to locate in the traditional area. Many extractive industries have no choice, having to be located by their materials (e.g. coal mines).

> The **cost of land** has become an increasingly important influence in making the location decision.

Some firms are heavily influenced by the **population distribution** of their final consumers: for instance, many firms supplying mass consumer goods locate production close to densely populated areas such as south-eastern England, though other influences (e.g. high property prices) may discourage this. Firms whose markets come to them, such as retail shops, have little choice but to be geographically dispersed. A related factor is the **image created for customers** by the location (e.g. the 'Harley Street specialist', and Bond and Regent Streets as London shopping areas).

Government

The UK government and the EU, through their development of **regional policies**, have become increasingly important influences. Government regional policy according to the DTI is to 'develop forward-looking regions by focusing support more on high-quality, knowledge-based projects which provide skilled jobs'.

> 'The Government is committed to creating a modern and competitive economy. Regional industrial policy has a key role to play. It brings under-utilised resources back into the economy, enhancing employment opportunities and improving competitiveness.' DTI, 2000

Figure 8.2 illustrates the new **Assisted Areas** recommended by the UK government. The availability of grants and other financial support have encouraged entrepreneurs to base their businesses in these areas where regional aid may be granted under EU law. This aid is discretionary, payable as a grant to secure employment opportunities and increase regional competitiveness and prosperity. 'Tier 1' areas are Cornwall, West Wales and the Valleys, Merseyside, and South Yorkshire. The 'Tier 2' areas also receive assistance.

> The four 'Tier 1' Assisted Areas were selected due to their GDP per head, which was below 75% of the EU average (1994/96).

The government has also proposed a third tier of **Enterprise Grant Areas,** where assistance will be available to businesses employing up to 250 people. These areas include:

- local authority districts with high unemployment
- coalfield areas
- Rural Development Areas.

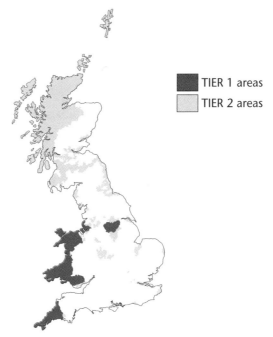

Figure 8.2 *UK map showing proposed Assisted Areas*   *Source: DTI 2000*

TIER 1 areas
TIER 2 areas

Personal and social influences

> There is geographical immobility of entrepreneurship, as well as of labour.

The personal preferences of the entrepreneur are important. Some entrepreneurs have ties to particular areas of the country, and may be unwilling to move elsewhere.

Pressure groups and others can influence a firm's location. Concern over factors such as the protection of natural habitats is an increasingly important influence, sometimes linked to a 'NIMBY' ('Not In My Back Yard') attitude to the location of those firms in less attractive industries such as waste disposal.

External economies

The existence of external economies of scale and concentration encourages firms to base their production in certain areas. For example, the UK car industry developed mainly in the Midlands, which led to a supply of skilled labour and component manufacturers in the area.

Locating internationally

Many of the above influences apply when an international decision is being made. Additional influences here are:

- the **exchange rate** – a history of highly fluctuating exchange rates will discourage an entrepreneur from locating in the country concerned
- **language and culture** – different cultural work habits and language communication problems are factors that may also discourage entrepreneurs
- **relative inflation** – an entrepreneur may be put off from locating in a country that traditionally suffers from high inflation levels
- **political climate** – countries with politically unstable regimes often find it difficult to encourage inward investment as a result of international location.

Making the decision

Decision-making techniques such as **investment appraisal** techniques (e.g. discounted cash flow) and **break-even analysis** can provide additional financial-based information to support any qualitative judgements made.

> Location decisions are influenced by quantitative (financial, cost and revenue) and qualitative (e.g. the entrepreneur's preferences) decisions.
>
> **KEY POINTS**

Progress check

1 List **three** influences on the location of a firm.

1 Government assistance; infrastructure (transport and communications); availability of sufficient and suitably skilled labour.

8.2 Developing operations

Research and development (R&D)

AQA	M5
EDEXCEL	M4
OCR	M7, M10
WJEC	M5
CEA	M5

The nature of R&D

Research explores the possibility of making new products and using new processes. **Development** turns this research into the new product or process.

R&D can be analysed into:

- **'pure'** research – original research to gain new knowledge or understanding, i.e. there is no obvious immediate commercial application
- **'applied'** research – also original research, but which has a practical application or aim in mind
- **development expenditure** – to produce new or substantially improved products or systems before starting commercial production.

> Applied research often focuses on researching how an existing product or system can be improved.

Since large companies spend significant amounts on these activities, R&D is often a major cost. Accountants either write off the R&D expenditure as an **expense**, or carry it forward as an **asset** and include it in the company's balance sheet. **SSAP 13** suggests that pure and applied research is written off as a cost in the relevant accounting period, because it is a continuing operation that helps ensure the company's survival. Development costs, however, may be treated as capital expenditure, and set off against future revenues associated with the project: the cost is spread over a number of financial periods.

> The accruals concept (page 79) justifies the spreading of development costs over a longer period of time.

	2000	*1999*	*1998*	*1997*	*1996*
R&D expenditure (£m)	345	268	307	291	282

Figure 8.3 *R&D expenditure by BT* Source: British telecommunications plc annual accounts, 2000

The R&D procedure

R&D is often associated with **new product development**. Here is the typical procedure for such development.

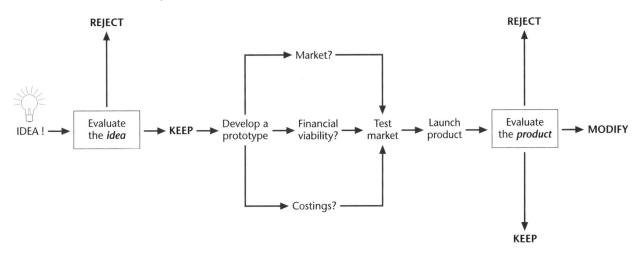

Figure 8.3 *The research and development procedure*

The research and development procedure may be halted at any time, because failure doesn't only occur at the beginning or end of this procedure.

The importance of R&D

The UK government is keen to ensure that British firms invest sufficiently in R&D, to ensure an international **competitive advantage**. In the UK, there is evidence that many firms may over-invest in their established business: whilst increased capital investment can improve productivity, it can also be at the expense of new activities.

Figure 8.4 summarises a DTI survey (2000), which suggests that many British leading manufacturers spend less on R&D than the international benchmark.

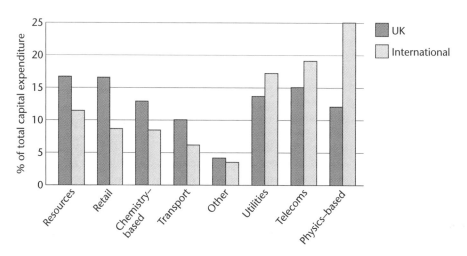

Figure 8.4 *UK and international spending on research*   *Source: DTI*

The conclusion from the DTI is that Britain's manufacturing sector in general invests two-thirds less (measured as pounds per employee) than international competitors. The following sectors were identified as particularly 'good' or 'bad':

Sectors above the benchmark	Sectors below the benchmark
Pharmaceutical; aerospace; defence	Automotive; chemical; information technology

Why is this important?

'Too many companies fail to recognise that research and development, capital investment and innovation are key drivers for business growth and competitiveness. Those that fail to invest will be left behind.'

Secretary of State for Trade and Industry, 2000

'Our people cannot cope competitively using yesterday's tools.'

Science and Innovation Minister, 2000

The conclusion can be drawn that:

- a lack of R&D may lead to **slower product development**, a **lack of innovation**, and **reduced competitiveness**; but
- more spending on R&D won't necessarily guarantee success
  - because it doesn't guarantee the **quality** of the R&D
  - and other factors are involved, e.g. the level of competition, exchange rate fluctuations for competitors, effects of government legislation.

Protecting the results of R&D

R&D may result in a profitable new product or system, i.e. some form of **invention** that will give the company a competitive advantage. To defend its invention, the company may:

- establish a **patent** (the sole right to use the invention, normally for 20 years)
- register the **design**, or
- register a **trade mark** – the feature that distinguishes the firm or its products from its competitors.

> If R&D is ignored, the firm risks losing future sales by over-concentrating on present sales.
>
> **KEY POINTS**

An example of R&D: the 'new generation jumbo'

> The Airbus A380 illustrates the economy of scale of increased dimensions.

The predicted growth in air travel (about 5% a year) encourages investment in research and development. For example, Airbus designed its new A380 'jumbo' at a development cost some have estimated as being up to £10 billion. Although only two metres longer and one metre higher than the best-selling Boeing 747, the new jumbo will save up to 20% fuel costs, and won't need a longer runway. This major commitment to research and development will probably change the nature and style of long-haul travel, but will also influence the travel policies of many countries, e.g. in how their airports cope with the expected increase in air travellers as a result of cheaper flights.

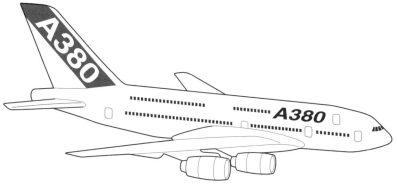

	New Airbus A380	**Boeing 747**
Seating capacity:	Up to 900	Up to 400
Length:	73 metres	71 metres
Height:	24.1 metres	19.4 metres
Range:	8 800 miles	8 400 miles

Figure 8.5 *The Airbus A380*

Progress check

1. Why is the level of research and development expenditure of interest to (a) an individual firm (b) the UK government?

1 (a) It indicates the amount of financial investment in the firm's future; (b) it provides a comparison against international R&D spending benchmarks.

8.3 Ensuring operational efficiency

After studying this section you should be able to:

- *explain the nature and relevance of critical path analysis*
- *calculate the critical path from given information*
- *outline the uses and limitations of ICT in making operations more efficient*

LEARNING SUMMARY

Critical path analysis

AQA A	M5
EDEXCEL	M4
OCR	M7, M10
WJEC	M5
CCEA	M5

> The CPA plan will only be as good as the staff's commitment to it.

CPA, also known as **network analysis**, is used to identify the best way of scheduling a complex series of related tasks, to minimise the time taken in their completion. It is widely used in industries such as construction, to schedule the different phases of planning and building. Most new and complex projects that take some time to complete can apply CPA techniques.

CPA allows planners to:

- forecast completion time for the project
- identify
  - EST (earliest start time)
  - EFT (earliest finish time)
  - LST (latest start time)
  - LFT (latest finish time)
- highlight all stages where timing is critical – the **critical path**
- monitor progress and delays throughout the project's life
- establish in advance the precise resources required
- identify ways to overcome resourcing and/or timing problems.

Stages in the construction of the network

1 Subdivide the project into its different activities. Each activity uses some resources, and takes some time to complete.

2 Decide on the order of completion. Some activities obviously precede others – e.g. building materials must obviously be bought before they can be used – although judgements often have to be made (for example, whether to plumb and fit a kitchen in a building before plumbing and fitting the bathroom). An activity may well depend on several preceding ones: e.g. 'install heating units' depends on activities such as 'wire room', 'install floor', 'plaster room' and so on.

3 Construct the network model and record the activity times.

4 Analyse the network. This establishes the total time for the project, and the critical path through it. This is the path where any delay to the activities also delays the whole project: there is no slack time. The total slack time, or 'float', represents the time the non-critical activities can over-run before they start delaying the project.

5 Draw up a timetable to schedule resources.

6 Monitor progress of the project by using the network.

> Because the CPA network of tasks is normally created by computer, the effect of changing variables such as the order in which the tasks are carried out can be evaluated.
>
> **KEY POINTS**

CPA: an illustration

The directors of a company wish to buy and assemble temporary additional office space. The activities are:

		Length (days)	Preceding activities
A	Obtain permission	3	—
B	Buy material for base	4	A
C	Obtain assembly	6	A
D	Lay base	3	B
E	Assemble office frame	5	C
F	Attach frame to base	2	D, E
G	Paint frame	2	C

Each activity is identified by a node represented by a circle (see figure 8.6). Nodes are numbered for identification, and represent the start and finish of an activity. They record the earliest start time (EST) and latest finish time (LFT) for each activity.

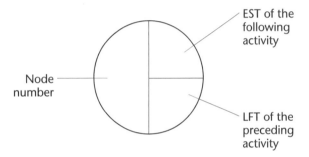

Figure 8.6 *Structure of the node*

Nodes are joined by arrows representing the flow of activities: the length of each arrow is not significant. Figure 8.7 shows the network model for the above activities. (In practice, the details by each arrow of the activity's name and length are usually omitted, but we show them here for reference.)

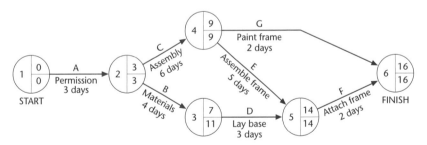

Figure 8.7 *The network diagram*

The EST represents the earliest date at which an activity can commence.

- Node 1 shows the start of activity A, which is day 0.
- Node 2 represents the start time for B and C. These must follow A, which takes three days to complete, so node 2 has an EST of day 3.
- Node 3 shows the start of activity D, which must follow B: B takes four days to complete, so node 3 has an EST of day 7.
- Node 4 represents the start of E and G, which follow the end of C: C takes six days, so E and G can't start before day 9.
- Node 5 shows the start of F, which follows the end of both D and E: the earliest D can end is after ten days (EST day 7 plus three days to complete), and the earliest E can finish is day 14 (EST day 9 + five days). Activity F can't start before both D and E are finished, so its EST is day 14.

- Node 6 ends with the finish of activities F (EST day 14 + two days) and G (EST day 9 + two days): so the whole project must take a minimum of 16 days.

The LFT represents the latest date by which an activity must be completed to avoid delaying the whole project. Each activity's LFT is calculated by *working backwards* **from the completion date.**

- Node 6 represents the end of the project, so its LFT must be 16 days.
- Node 5 shows the start of activity F, which takes two days to complete: the LFT for activities D and E shown by this node is therefore (16 – 2 =) day 14.
- Node 4 starts activity G, which takes two days: the LFT is not (16 – 2) day 14, because node 4 also starts activity E. This activity takes five days and has an LFT of day 14 shown in node 5. The LFT for node 4 must be (14 – 5 =) day 9.
- Node 3 starts activity D, with an LFT of 14 shown in node 5: D takes 3 days to complete, so the LFT for activity B which precedes it is (14 – 3 =) day 11.
- Node 2 represents the LFT for activity A. Although activity B could start on day 7 (it takes 4 days and its LFT is day 11), activity C's LFT is day 9 (node 4) and it takes six days to complete. The LFT for activity A is day 3 (9 – 6).
- Node 1 represents the start of the project and has an LFT of day 0: the LFT at the start must be the same as the EST.

The critical path can now be seen. It is shown by those nodes with the same EST and LFT: 1, 2, 4, 5 and 6. Any delay in the activities they represent (A, C, E and F) will delay the project as a whole. Activities B, D and G are non-critical because they can over-run without the project being delayed. They have 'floats' that indicate the spare time available to complete them.

- Activity B could be delayed without affecting the project: its EST is day 3, but it could start later to meet its LFT of day 11. It has a float, which is calculated by deducting its earliest start time from its latest start time (LST – EST). The LST in turn is calculated by taking an activity's duration from its LFT. For activity B: the LST is day 7 (11 – 4); the EST is day 3; its float is four days.

Eight days could therefore be taken to complete B without the project being delayed.

- Activity D also has a float of four days: Its LST is day 11 and its EST is day 7.
- Activity G has a float of five days: its LST is day 14 and its EST is day 9.

By using CPA and establishing the critical path, managers make their planning more efficient. For example, CPA allows them to time the placing of orders, and to identify those events in a project that can be carried out simultaneously.

The **Gantt chart**, a form of horizontal bar chart showing each activity as a bar against time, is an alternative form of display.

CPA is used as a **control technique**: in particular, it controls **time** and **working capital**.

KEY POINTS

Using ICT

AQA	M5
EDEXCEL	M4
OCR	M7, M10
WJEC	M5
CCEA	M5

According to the ONS, the mobile phone industry grew by over 40% from 1999 to 2000.

ICT – **Information (and) Communications Technology** – applications in business are widespread and always evolving. Two important recent developments are:

- the Internet as (a) a source of information, and (b) an advertising and selling outlet in its **e-commerce** form
- the creation of new industries, or adaptation of existing ones, such as the mobile 'phone and telecommunications industries.

Figure 8.8 summarises the typical use of ICT for an individual firm.

Application	Database	Spreadsheet
Feature	Store, search and manipulate volume data stored as fields within records.	Store, search and manipulate numerical data, and display it in summary forms.
Typical uses	Customer records, e.g. age and amount of debts; customer spending patterns (e.g. Tesco and other storecard data); suppliers' and stock records; personnel records.	Financial management, e.g. cash flow forecasting, budgetary control (variance calculations); analysis of sales statistics and market research data; calculation of EOQ in purchasing.

Figure 8.8 *The use of ICT applications by function*

The 1998 Data Protection Act controls the nature and accessibility of data stored both electronically and manually.

Other ICT applications within the firm include:

- **word processing** (e.g. letters) and **email** for correspondence
- **EPOS** – electronic point of sale, used in retailing where product data is captured scanning the bar code, and sent to a computer, to update stock records and create a new order required
- **CAD/CAM** systems, often linked to **manufacturing resource planning** software so that the proposed new product's cost can be calculated.

email and the Internet

The European online advertising market was expected to reach £1 billion by 2001 and £3.6 billion by 2004, according to online advertising company 24/7 Media Inc.

The Internet has grown dramatically as a source of information and trade. Its growth is helped by the fact that it can be relatively cheap to establish an Internet site. With the use of email, a two-way correspondence will exist, with customers able to place an order and arrange payment electronically.

Limitations of ICT

The DTI's **UK online for business** provides businesses with advice on using ICT.

- ICT is only a support tool – it cannot by itself make decisions and solve problems. Its effective use relies on how managers use it.
- An efficient ICT system requires correct selection of hardware and software, efficient installation and continuing technical support, and effective staff training in its use.

Although there is a rapid pace of change with ICT hardware and software, the functions and tasks they support, and the way they make these more efficient, remain essentially the same.

KEY POINTS

Key points from AS

- **E-commerce**
  Revise AS pages 115–116
- **The role of technology in productive efficiency**
  Revise AS page 125

Progress check

1 What is the purpose of critical path analysis?

2 .How could (a) spreadsheets, (b) databases, (c) word processing and (d) the Internet make the work of a marketing department more efficient?

1 To show the optimum way to schedule a range of related tasks, to minimise time taken.

2 (a) To analyse sales statistics; (b) to store customer information; (c) to produce sales literature; (d) to advertise and sell via a company's website.

Sample question and model answer

1

Read this article and answer the questions that follow.

> **Nissan in the North-east**
>
> In the 1990s a new industry – vehicles – grew up in the north-east of England, centred on Nissan's purpose-built production plant in Sunderland. Nissan invested some £700 million, and employed about 5000 workers. Its production was aimed at both the UK and export markets, including the EU, Japan and the Far East.
>
> The decision by Nissan to invest led to a development in the region of vehicle component suppliers. Joint ventures were also set up to produce components such as plastic mouldings, tyres and car seats.

(a) What factors are likely to have encouraged Nissan to establish its plant at Sunderland? [6]

(b) Nissan decided to produce in the UK for export, rather than establishing plants in several other countries where it planned to sell its vehicles. Examine the benefits and drawbacks of this approach. [8]

(c) What factors would influence Nissan's decision to 'buy-in' components rather than to make them itself? [6]

(a) It is likely that Nissan was offered some financial incentive by the British Government to locate in the north-east. This is because the area has suffered from a lack of investment, and there was high unemployment there. It doesn't mean, however, that the workers in the region have the relevant skills for Nissan, so it may need to do a lot of training. Since Nissan is an exporter, it would have wanted to make sure it could export its vehicles easily, so transport lines and general communication lines needed to be good. This also applies when importing its raw materials. Finally, Nissan would have considered where its suppliers are based, perhaps being influenced by the UK's history of making vehicles and building the components to go in them.

Valid points are made, but the decline in the traditional industries (e.g. mining and shipbuilding) could also be mentioned as supporting evidence. Also, the fact that Nissan produced vehicles in the UK meant that, as a member of the EU, the Common External Tariff would be avoided when exporting to other EU countries.

(b) Nissan gains from economies of scale. A single plant is capable of greater mass production, so unit costs could well be lower than if it had several factories making the same vehicles. These economies would include technical economies such as using specialist equipment like welding equipment or computerised robots doing some assembly tasks. Also, financial economies, marketing economies and purchasing economies are likely to exist.

The answer ignores the drawbacks and also would be strengthened by providing more illustrations: e.g. (financial) borrowing at lower cost, (marketing) centralised marketing function is less costly than one at each plant, and bulk-buying (purchasing).

(c) By making the components itself, Nissan has greater control. It can also reduce costs, because the suppliers have the expertise and can make the components efficiently, store them for Nissan, and deliver them when needed. There are likely to be hundreds of different components in a vehicle, so it would be very complicated for Nissan to co-ordinate all this production. The problem it may have faced involves ensuring the quality of what the suppliers are making. Also, failure by one supplier could halt production.

The answer could refer to the strengths and weaknesses of the 'Just-in-time' approach, and also to Nissan avoiding some other (e.g. R&D) costs, which could be borne by the component suppliers.

Practice examination questions

1 Carnival Ltd needs to plan the time required to manufacture its product, which goes through nine processes. Each process takes the following number of hours to complete:

Process	Time (hours)
A	6
B	4
C	15
D	10
E	8
F	6
G	3
H	9
I	4

(a) Complete the network to show the EST and LFT for each activity, and the critical path. [6]

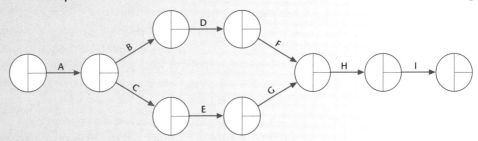

(b) Outline the advantages of using CPA. [4]

2 'An organisation in the 21st century cannot hope to succeed without effective use of ICT.'

Discuss this statement. [8]

Chapter 9

Synoptic assessment

The nature of synoptic assessment in Business Studies

All Business Studies A Level specifications have to include a minimum of 20% '**synoptic assessment**'. These Business Studies specifications encourage students to see the **relationship** between different aspects of this subject. To achieve this, the synoptic assessment you face draws together everything you've learnt. It relates to **all** your assessment objectives by **integrating** the knowledge, understanding and skills you've studied in the different parts of the Advanced GCE course.

You have four assessment objectives. These are described on page 10. You need to:

* demonstrate your **knowledge** and **understanding** of the content
* **apply** this knowledge and understanding to problems and issues from familiar and unfamiliar situations
* **analyse** these problems and issues
* **evaluate** (make judgements).

How are you assessed using this synoptic approach? The method used in Business Studies is to give you a **case study**, through which you're asked to apply your Business Studies knowledge, understanding and skills to the case situation. You will meet decision-making and problem-solving type questions, based on the case situation or context, that require you to make and justify your decisions or solve the given business problems.

The ways in which the exam boards are tackling synoptic assessment are to have synoptic modules or units worth 20% of the overall weighting, with case study assessment as follows.

* **AQA**'s Module 6 'External Influences and Objectives and Strategy' requires candidates to answer a number of compulsory questions based on a 1 hour 30 minute case study.
* **OCR**'s 'Business Strategy' unit is synoptic, having a pre-issued case study with a written paper (2 hours) containing four compulsory questions.
* **Edexcel**'s Unit 6 'Corporate Strategy' has a synoptic paper, a pre-seen case study with compulsory questions lasting 1 hour 30 minutes.
* **WJEC** has an assessment unit consisting of an examination paper lasting 1 hour 45 minutes, with questions based on a case study.
* **CCEA** assesses its four taught modules synoptically with a 1 hour 40 minute exam based on an unseen case study.

Example of synoptic assessment

Here's an example of a synoptic-style case study.

Answer the **one** question in this section.

Olympic plc

1   Olympic plc will celebrate 40 years in business in March 2001. The business has undergone many changes since it was established and the next few years seem certain to bring even more. The business was founded in Strabane by Adam Watts who originally produced high-quality shoes for ladies. These were entirely hand-made, often to order, and were very expensive. The business quickly gained a reputation for quality products.

2   Over the years additional machinery was introduced into the production process and the business began to diversify from just producing ladies' shoes. A range of shoes for men was also developed, as well as the

CASE STUDY

manufacture of training shoes. All of these products were manufactured using production lines. They were standardised and aimed at mass markets.

3   The business was incorporated in 1971 and went public in 1978 in order to raise capital for the purchase of its present factory, still in Strabane. At that time, the decision was taken to concentrate solely on the manufacture of training shoes, upon which Olympic plc has built its current reputation. The main person behind this new strategy was Sean Watts, Marketing Manager and son of the founder. Having recently graduated from university with a marketing degree, Sean impressed everyone with his analytical skills and leadership ability. He is currently the Managing Director of the Company.

4   The strategy of concentrating solely on the manufacture of training shoes was very successful. A single style of training shoe was mass produced cheaply and sold to a rapidly growing market under the brand name Olympians. Almost all sales were through sports shops with the remainder being sold through shoe shops. The trainers were promoted extensively so that the brand quickly gained national recognition as a top-quality product, meeting the requirements of serious sportsmen and sportswomen. Over the years famous international athletes have been used to advertise Olympians. Although styles and materials have evolved, especially in recent years, the factory continues to make a single style of training shoe which is sold using the Olympians brand name.

Recent years

5   Olympic plc has been experiencing some difficulties. The market growth rate has slowed down and sales have been hit by competition from other brands in this highly competitive market. Some other companies manufacture their trainers overseas using cheap labour and employ penetration pricing strategies. Prestige pricing has been used for Olympians but this may not always be possible in the future. Research into the price elasticity of demand for Olympians has indicated that the demand for them appears to be becoming more elastic. Last year a 3% price increase caused monthly sales to fall by 5%.

6   The share price of the company has been fluctuating and now seems to be on a downward trend. This has led to some unease among major shareholders who are worried about their long-term investment in the company. Undoubtedly, external factors have played their part in these share price fluctuations. Fortunately the business has considerable cash reserves, built up during periods of sustained profits, so dividends have, so far, been maintained at a satisfactory level.

Product quality

7   For about four years there has been concern that quality standards in the factory are slipping. Initially, these problems were on a small scale but if the trend is not reversed soon it could damage the reputation of the Olympians brand name amongst customers, many of whom make repeat purchases. The brand relies heavily on its quality image to appeal to its target segment. Any bad publicity in this area would have serious repercussions for sales in the future.

8   There has been no underlying pattern to these returns. They are not confined to any group of retailers or time of the year. Various parts of the trainers have been found to be defective on different occasions. Materials used in manufacture were found to be of satisfactory quality. Most of the complaints have been concerned with faults in the assembly of the trainers, although no single stage of the production process has been identified as being at fault. It would appear to be a factory-wide problem.

Average number of pairs of Olympians returned to the factory per 1000 sold

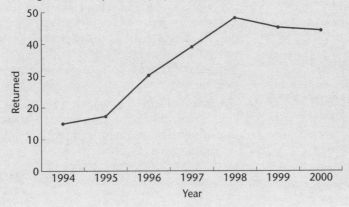

Table 1 illustrates the growing problem of Olympians being returned. This is currently being used as a measure of product quality. The 2000 figure is an estimate for the year, based on performance to date.

CASE STUDY

Attempted solutions

9 Various attempts have been made to tackle this issue in Olympic plc. In February 1996, considerable restructuring took place within the company. Job enrichment was used as a means of motivating workers who were becoming bored with their jobs. An attempt was made to improve working conditions in parts of the factory by redecorating workshops and by upgrading some machinery. Workers were pleased with these changes but by June 1997 no overall improvement in quality standards had been achieved.

TQM

10 In October 1997, the Operations Manager, Margaret Wilkinson, approached Sean Watts, the Managing Director, and requested that a system of Total Quality Management (TQM) be introduced into the factory. She hoped that by putting more emphasis on quality chains within the business, all workers would come to recognise that their individual roles in the production process were important and this would lead to an overall improvement in performance. Margaret also hoped that it would provide a system to measure improvements in performance over time.

11 At first Sean Watts was not convinced of the need to introduce a whole factory solution to what he regarded as a production line problem. As he read more about the benefits of TQM however, he too became convinced that it would be beneficial to Olympic plc. He formed a steering group made up of departmental managers to take responsibility for the immediate introduction of TQM. Most of the managers were enthusiastic although there were a few sceptics. After two months this group had produced a company quality policy. This was distributed to all workers in January 1998 at a formal ceremony to launch TQM.

12 At this ceremony Sean Watts explained the philosophy of TQM to the workforce and emphasised that it is the role and commitment of every worker which will make the policy a success. The mood was very positive. Over the year there were many changes in the factory. Departmental working groups examined processes and made plans for improvements. New statistical process controls were introduced. However, the number of Olympians returned to the factory fell only slightly and workers began to complain about the increasing amount of documentation required and the continuous audits which took place.

13 In 1999, training for workers was increased even though it cost more than originally planned. Despite this increased cost, the steering group was provided with all the funds it needed to achieve its objectives. By the end of the year there was a marginal improvement in the number of Olympians returned. Some workers still complained of having to work harder but the mood in the factory was generally still positive.

Tech 2000

14 In February 2000, Peter Bradley, the Marketing Manager, read the section in the quality policy document about 'meeting customer requirements'. He decided to investigate if this was happening. While analysing sales information he became aware that a growing percentage of company sales were being made, not through sports shops, but through shoe shops. This led Peter to believe that a significant proportion of all customers were buying trainers for fashion purposes rather than for sport. Market research confirmed this view.

15 Peter was convinced that this new market segment of wearing trainers as a fashion item should be targeted separately with another brand of trainers. In his opinion, prices could be more easily raised in this segment. He put a proposal to the Board of Directors of Olympic plc that a new brand of trainers, Tech 2000, should be created with a modern, fashionable image, well away from the sporty one of Olympians. These would be sold mainly in shoe shops, competing against casual footwear. The Olympians brand would, of course, continue to be produced.

16 The production of the new brand would require additional machinery but Peter had researched all available possibilities. Having consulted with Margaret Wilkinson, the Operations Manager, he proposed siting the new machines in an old unused warehouse adjacent to the factory. This had just come up for sale and could probably be purchased at a low cost given current market conditions. It could then be easily and cheaply converted for the purpose.

17 Peter was able to produce figures to show that buying and equipping the warehouse would lead to a significant increase in the cash flow of the business after four years, even when using pessimistic sales projections. However, Olympic plc would initially have the opportunity cost of other planned property purchases. The business may have liquidity problems if the decision was made to undertake both projects.

18 The Board of Directors were impressed by Peter's research and made a decision to enter this new market segment and produce Tech 2000 trainers, as Peter had proposed. Sean Watts was a happy man. Things were certainly looking up for Olympic plc.

Sample question and model answer

1

(a) (i)   Explain what is meant by Olympians having an elastic demand.   [2]

   (ii)   What factors might have caused the demand for Olympians to be elastic?   [2]

   (iii)   Explain the implications of this elastic demand for the future pricing strategy of Olympic plc.   [4]

(b) How might Peter Bradley, the Marketing Manager, have carried out market research to estimate the size of the Northern Ireland market for Tech 2000, the new brand of trainers?   [8]

(c) Evaluate the attempt made to introduce TQM into Olympic plc. How successful do you think the system is likely to be in the long term?   [16]

(d) (i)   Explain what is meant by the term cash flow in Olympic plc.   [2]

   (ii)   How might Olympic plc ensure they do not experience a cash flow crisis when they buy and equip the warehouse?   [10]

(e) Evaluate the decision of Olympic plc to begin producing Tech 2000, the new brand of trainers.   [16]

CCEA 2000, GCE A Level, Business Studies, paper 2

You will find the suggested answers to these case study questions in the Answers section on page 142.

In this case study, the range of **content** includes supply and demand, pricing and market research, quality issues, cash flow, and production. The major Business Studies areas taught – accounting and finance, HRM, marketing and production – all feature, together with the external environment (supply and demand, pricing, market research) and internal organisation of the company.

How do the **skills** required to answer this case study relate to the four assessment objectives (page 10)? You have to:

- **explain** – e.g. by demonstrating your Business Studies knowledge and understanding of key terms and concepts such as 'elastic demand' – and apply this knowledge (in part (a) (ii) you apply the idea of elastic demand to Olympic's situation)
- **analyse** – examine a problem or situation, and break it down into its different parts (e.g. part (d) (ii) asks you to analyse Olympic's cash flow situation)
- **make decisions and judgements** – e.g. in part (e) you evaluate (make a judgement about) a given decision.

Sample question and model answer (continued)

Each of the four assessment objectives can be classified into **levels**. A four-stage 'levels of response' approach is then used to structure the questions and the marking scheme: the higher the level achieved, the more marks awarded. For example, AQA's approach to the four levels of Knowledge and Understanding is:

Level			
1	2	3	4
Includes some relevant materials and shows some understanding, but lacking clarity, focus and depth	Includes relevant material, presented appropriately, and showing understanding but lacking clarity, focus and depth	Includes relevant material, fully explained and presented appropriately, but lacking focus	Includes relevant materials, focused clearly on the project objective(s), fully explained and presented appropriately

You will also be assessed on the **quality of your written communication**, and the synoptic case study may be used as part of this assessment. The criteria you'll be judged on are your ability to:

- select and use an **appropriate writing style**
- **organise** the written information clearly, using **specialist business language** appropriately
- write legibly, using accurate '**SPG**' (spelling, punctuation and grammar).

Practice examination answers

Chapter 1 The external environment

1 (a) Finance: investment in 'environmentally friendly' equipment, possible cash flow problems. Personnel: employee training, greater employee awareness, increased public relations responsibility. Marketing: influencing advertising/selling policy, need to create consumer awareness of changes, alterations in packaging policy. Production: lower economies of scale, products less standardised in nature, increased production costs, more expensive quality control, manufacturing with new materials, discontinuing some processes and ingredients, adds to research and development costs. Other: facing fines for pollution/other offences.

(b) Social costs, borne by the community through the actions of the firm; increased pollution through burning. Financial costs: capital expenditure (purchase of machinery), revenue expenditure (depreciation of machinery, wages to operate it, maintenance, etc.). Opportunity cost: the cost of the alternatives required to land-fill, and the cost to the firm of buying the machinery (this capital expenditure is not available for different uses).

2 (a) No currency conversion costs when receiving payment from EU importers, since the euro is the trading currency. No uncertainty from fluctuating exchange rates, therefore better able to plan exporting in greater certainty. Enables the existing customs union to operate even more efficiently, saving the exporter costs and time. A 'level playing field' is created for all competitors, so the UK exporter is not disadvantaged in any way.

(b) Many UK exporters believe that the euro will enable them to compete on equal terms with other exporters in the euro area. Others may not support the euro because they believe that retaining the pound gives the UK government greater opportunity to support exporters through competitive action (e.g. devaluing the pound if necessary).

Chapter 2 Business organisations

1 (a) The 'number of employees' is only one of several indicators that can be used to measure a firm's size. It may give a misleading indication of size.

(i) Some industries (e.g. chemicals) are capital-intensive and others (e.g. tourism) are labour-intensive: firms that are the same size when measured by, say, capital employed or turnover, can have greatly differing employee levels.

(ii) Within a single industry, the level of technology varies: a firm replacing labour with capital might be growing and yet have a falling number of employees.

(iii) 'Employees' needs defining: one firm might include only productive and direct support (office) employees, whereas another could count part-time staff, cleaners, etc. There can be a lack of consistency in whom to include.

(iv) Some industries (e.g. agriculture, tourism) face large seasonal fluctuations in their workforce: when does the count take place?

(b) The small-firm sector remains important because it:

(i) contributes to the UK's balance of payments through exporting

(ii) often provides service support to larger firms

(iii) can adapt and respond quickly to changing conditions

(iv) fills gaps in the economy where larger firms may not operate (e.g. meeting local demand)

(v) may act as a 'seed-bed' of ideas and developments.

Chapter 3 Business objectives

1 (a) This occurs when an organisation prepares for unplanned eventualities. Typical situations include preparing for a possible general economic downturn/recession, or a sudden change in demand due to a specific event such as the financial collapse of a customer, or a competitor introducing a technological development.

(b) Contingency planning will be expensive because it tends to be based on computer modelling, the computer program answering 'what if?' questions. Contingency planning will help identify weaknesses such as over-reliance on a single supplier or customer: as a result, the organisation can take appropriate action (e.g. use another supplier, diversify into another market/segment). By doing so, the risk of a future major problem is reduced, and – as a result – the organisation may regard the investment in contingency planning as a form of 'insurance'.

Chapter 4 Corporate culture

1 (a) Their skills may be highly demanded and in short supply: as a result, the price of their labour will be high. They provide leadership for a company, e.g. by representing it in its relationships with the outside world, e.g. at meetings with the media and shareholders: they also represent it internally when liaising with unions or employees. They provide motivation for internal (e.g. employee) and external (e.g. shareholder) groups, through effective leadership, establishment and communication of the company's policy. They set the company's strategic plan, and help translate it into achievable objectives.

(b) A democratic management role normally creates motivated employees, and encourages them to work harder. There is likely to be good communication, and the managers will be in a position to explain their high incomes: with a democratic role, they would probably be expected to justify these incomes. The democratic style normally means that employees are aware of, and support, the organisation's objectives: these objectives should support the sort of pay discrepancies that occur when managers receive high pay. Some employees may find the existence of highly paid top managers demotivating, and this could influence their work and be communicated through the hierarchy/chain of command.

Chapter 5 Marketing

1 (a) The image of the person (should be appropriate for the product's target audience); the cost of the person (compared to the relative fame of the person and the degree of their involvement in promoting the product).

(b) Price is an indicator of the product's 'utility' (worth) to the purchaser, but there are three other elements in the marketing mix: the effectiveness of promotion, the efficiency of distribution (place) and the quality and other attributes of the product all play their part in bringing success. Also, effective product differentiation and other forms of non-price competition allow sellers to compete successfully, e.g. by using the differentiated 'unique features' to target their products at particular segments.

(c) Since L'Oreal is a global business, it will need to consider international influences in addition to national ones: for example, different legal and technical requirements (e.g. product information required) in foreign markets, and different political influences. In particular, it will need to consider changes in language (e.g. product labelling), national culture and local tastes (e.g. acceptance of the use of hair products, views on colours used in packaging), and the comparative stage of development of the society and its economy.

Chapter 6 Accounting and finance

1 The act of going through the budgeting process will encourage Leigh and Arthur to co-ordinate the various business activities, and will provide the main element of financial control they will need, especially considering their plans to expand.

Since budgeting provides a financial plan of the business's future, it could help Leigh and Arthur by indicating the capital cost of the proposed new premises and machinery, and the cost of wages/salaries for the new staff. 'Rent or buy' decisions will have to be made regarding the premises and machinery, i.e. whether capital or revenue expenditure is involved. The budget (e.g. a cash flow forecast) will provide a clear indication of the cash flows involved, when financing is required, and the level of that finance. This in turn will suggest an appropriate source for the finance.

2 (i) Gearing refers to the relationship between 'prior charge' capital (the 'fixed-interest' capital such as debentures and other long-term loans, and preference shares) and equity (ordinary shares). A highly-geared company is one having over 50% prior charge capital.

(ii)(a) $\dfrac{1\ 500\ 000}{7\ 500\ 000} \times 100 = 20\%$

(b) I would be happy with the level of gearing. Delphware is a low-geared company and therefore loses comparatively small amounts of its income in the form of interest payments. This means there will be more net profit available for the ordinary shareholders. Also, the company is a relatively low-risk business in which to invest, because it has to meet relatively small interest payments, and so there is less chance that it will face financial difficulty through not being able to pay interest.

(iii) By finding an additional £900 000 loan finance, Delphware's gearing ratio will change: £2.4 million as a percentage of £8.4 million (28.6%). The ratio still shows it as a 'low-geared' business, and so the risk factor hasn't increased substantially, although this ratio should be benchmarked against the industry average. If the alternative is to issue ordinary shares, as things stand the company cannot make an additional issue (Issued Capital = Authorised Capital): it would need to increase the amount of its authorised capital. Issuing additional ordinary shares risks losing an element of control, since the ordinary shareholders can vote: debenture

Chapter 6 Accounting and finance (continued)

holders, as lenders, don't have such a direct control in the company's affairs. Another benefit to the company is that debenture interest is paid out of untaxed (gross) profit, whereas ordinary share dividends have to be paid from taxed net profit.

The drawbacks of issuing debentures are that the company's commitment to paying interest is increased substantially: interest payments would, apparently, almost double. The company would need to check its interest cover ratio to establish by how many times its operating profit (profit before interest and tax) 'covered' its interest payments. There is a requirement to repay debenture capital in the future – this is not so with ordinary shares – and therefore the company will need to take this into account.

As regards leasing the new machinery, one important fact is that Delphware will never own the assets concerned. Perhaps the main advantage is that it does not have to pay out a large capital sum: this helps its liquidity position, and any sum that is available could be reinvested and/or used for future capital expenditure. Other advantages are that it can more easily update its assets, and there is no depreciation to take into account. The main disadvantage is that it never owns the assets concerned, which are therefore not shown in its balance sheet. Also, it will have to meet regular payments in the future, thereby possibly affecting its future liquidity position.

Chapter 7 People in organisations

1 Shareholder and profit-sharing schemes bring with them the feeling of greater involvement, owning a share of the firm's success and having a direct benefit (profit) from direct involvement (work). However, like all financial rewards these schemes are of limited motivational value only, since theorists such as Maslow and Herzberg have identified the importance of non-financial factors in motivating staff. Large companies such as Tesco acknowledge this, using other motivational approaches such as job enrichment.

2 (a) For employers, there will be enhanced performance at work by staff; as a result, costs should fall/output should rise. Staff are also likely to be more loyal,

thereby reducing labour turnover and associated costs. For employees, it should be easier to accommodate work and domestic/leisure time, thereby improving motivation and commitment, and possibly leading to higher pay (e.g. through greater efficiency).

(b) Employees have a point of contact who can advise them/put them in touch with experts. The grievance procedure will have been agreed between the parties, and union staff will ensure these procedures are followed, and that they occur within any set time limits. Employees also gain from 'moral support' as well as union expertise, and management is likely to take the grievance more seriously.

Chapter 8 Operations management

1 (a)

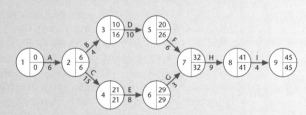

Activity	Duration	EST	LFT
A	6	0	6
B	4	6	16
C	15	6	21
D	10	10	26
E	8	21	29
F	6	20	32
G	3	29	32
H	9	32	41
I	4	41	45

The critical path is where EST = LFT, i.e. nodes 1, 2, 4, 6, 7, 8, 9.

(b) The 'critical time', i.e. where there is no slack production time, is now known. Any time lost in any of these processes will affect the overall time spent in production. This allows the firm to prioritise and to ensure the processes run smoothly. Efficiency is therefore improved.

2 ICT's importance is recognised, e.g. in making communication more efficient and in providing tools (e.g. spreadsheets) to assist decision-making. For example, ICT brings almost instantaneous information into the business, and the speed and power of computer-based applications software means it can be used to quickly translate data into meaningful information. As a result, the firm may gain a competitive advantage.

ICT has a role to play in all functional areas: e.g. marketing (databases for market research), finance (analysis of variances), purchasing (calculation of EOQ), production (scheduling of production runs).

Two limitations need considering: (a) it is only a support tool, and cannot by itself make decisions and solve problems; and (b) how efficient the firm's ICT system is depends on factors such as correct selection of hardware/software, efficient installation, suitable technical support, and adequate staff training in its use.

Chapter 9 Synoptic assessment

(a) (i) The case study refers to price elasticity, which measures the responsiveness of the quantity being demanded to price changes. The fact that Olympians have an elastic demand means that their demand is responsive to price, i.e. a small change in price brings about a larger change in quantity demanded.

(ii) Elastic demand is often found where there are a large number of alternative (substitute) products, normally sold in a highly competitive market. The product itself is likely to be a luxury rather than a necessity ('necessity' products tend to have inelastic demand).

(iii) Because a price change results in a greater change in quantity demanded, Olympic will find that a price cut should increase overall sales revenue (higher % being sold) and a price rise will reduce overall revenue. Overall profits should increase from a price cut, assuming profit margins aren't tight (unlikely given the prestige pricing policy). Its pricing strategy will become more competitive.

(b) Peter Bradley could use either primary ('field') or secondary ('desk') research. Ideally, he will be able to use both approaches, to give a more complete picture. For primary research he will need to establish the sample size and sampling method (e.g. random, quota-based). He must also consider how to collect the data: e.g. by interview face-to-face, or questionnaire completion by customers. Cost may be a limiting factor here. If Peter decides to use desk research, he can examine government (ONS) supplied statistics, e.g. on population age trends and spending patterns. Other sources include specialist market reports, or from analysing published information from competitors (e.g. their annual report and accounts). These are sources external to the firm: internal sources include sales and other statistics that will be available. Although typically less costly than field research, this data will not have been collected and displayed with Peter Bradley's purposes in mind, and may therefore be of limited relevance only.

(c) To implement TQM successfully, there need to be clear statements, communication and policy related to company objectives. All staff must be prepared to commit themselves to the TQM approach, i.e. to take responsibility for maintaining, and for seeking to improve, quality. The case study contains evidence that TQM was introduced successfully and efficiently: e.g. support of the Managing Director, acknowledgment that TQM is factory-wide and affects everyone, the explanation to (and positive outlook of) the staff, creation of the steering group leading to overall manager support, and a quality policy being established. There is also evidence of suitable review and modification: e.g. increased training, a willingness to meet additional costs, the positive mood retained. However, there is also more negative evidence: not all managers are convinced of TQM's value, the number of staff complaints about documentation and audits which continue, the increased cost of training, no clear evidence that TQM has dramatically improved quality of product. This would suggest that, to this point, the introduction of TQM has been partially successful. It is too early to reach a clear judgement, especially since TQM can take years to become fully embedded into a company and to have a full effect on its quality.

(d) (i) Cash flow is a record of all cash movements in a business, whether on revenue expenditure (paying bills) or capital expenditure (purchase of fixed assets), or received from trading or from additional finance/sale of surplus assets.

(ii) Olympic needs to examine cash linked to their assets, liabilities and production. Assets: (current) increase stock turnover by reducing stocks and only make essential purchases, examine efficiency of credit control and consider factoring debts, (fixed) consider credit sale, sale/leaseback or normal leasing to avoid large cash outlays, sell any surplus fixed assets. Liabilities: check 'creditor days' to ensure credit being taken, seek credit facilities. Production system: use JIT to control stock supply and storage costs. Control system: budgetary control will help forecast cash movements. Overall, the company needs to ensure that, by avoiding cash difficulties, it does not get into production difficulties: e.g. JIT takes time to establish (relationships with suppliers, etc.), and sale of assets that are not surplus to requirements may cause production problems.

(e) (General arguments) Producing Tech 2000 allows the company to diversify, and spread risk by selling another product in a different market segment. (Financial) Overall sales will increase, and – if prices can be raised as the case study suggests – there should be substantial profit due to the higher profit margin available. Any investment takes time to recoup its outlay, so the company needs to ensure it is financially able to support the investment. The company seems to be stable financially and in cash terms, so the financial risk can be taken. The shareholders may find the share price improves, now there is evidence of longer-term planning and development of new products. (Marketing) The existing Olympian product is well known, so the positive brand name can be used to support the new product. Each product is also at a different stage in its life cycle, which is good for the overall product portfolio. (HRM) Starting to produce a new product is often motivating for the staff involved. (Production) Increased production may well bring economies of scale for the company.

However, the company hasn't resolved the problems of quality related to its existing products. The possible reaction of competitors needs analysing. (Financial) The new product requires heavy promotion, which can be costly. The cost of the old warehouse is not stated, and may be higher than first thought. (Marketing) There is no guarantee that the market research data is accurate. (HRM) Training will be required, which is costly and may disrupt current production. (Production) The new factory extension may disrupt present production.

Given the company's present situation, the production of Tech 2000 is probably justified on the evidence available.

38002013674025.

Index